LOUIE GIGLIO

WITH STUART HALL

STUDENT EDITION OF **THE AIR I BREATHE**

FOR A LIFE OF WORSHIP

LEADER'S GUIDE

MULTNOMAH PUBLISHERS® *Sisters, Oregon*

published by Multnomah Publishers

A division of Random House, Inc.

© 2006 by Louie Giglio
International Standard Book Number: 1-59052-607-4

Design: Kirk DouPonce, DogEaredDesign.com
Photography: Stepen Gardner, PixelWorks Studios, www.shootpw.com
Journey illustrations: Deeann Carson

Unless otherwise indicated, Scripture quotations are from:
New American Standard Bible © 1960, 1977, 1995
by the Lockman Foundation. Used by permission.
Other Scripture quotations are from:
The Holy Bible, New International Version (NIV)
© 1973, 1984 by International Bible Society,
used by permission of Zondervan Publishing House
The Message © 1993, 1994, 1995, 1996, 2000, 2001, 2002
Used by permission of NavPress Publishing Group
The Holy Bible, King James Version (KJV)
All Scripture quotations in the *30-Day Worship Journey* are from:
The Holy Bible, New International Version (NIV)
© 1973, 1984 by International Bible Society,
used by permission of Zondervan Publishing House
Multnomah is a trademark of Multnomah Publishers and is registered in the U.S. Patent and Trademark Office.
The colophon is a trademark of Multnomah Publishers.

Printed in China

For information:
MULTNOMAH PUBLISHERS
12265 ORACLE BOULEVARD, SUITE 200 • COLORADO SPRINGS, CO 80921

LIBRARY OF CONGRESS CATALOGING-IN-PUBLICATION DATA
Giglio, Louie.
   Wired : for a life of worship / Louie Giglio with Stuart Hall.
      p. cm.
   Includes bibliographical references and index.
   ISBN 1-59052-607-4 (alk. paper)
1. Self-actualization--Religious aspects--Christianity. 2. Vocation—
Christianity. 3. Worship. I. Hall, Stuart. II. Title.
   BV4598.2.G54 2006
   248.3--dc22
          2005028995

06 07 08 09 10—10 9 8 7 6 5 4 3 2 1

TABLE OF CONTENTS

In order to help the leader expand on Louie's lessons, each chapter begins with a Wired Connection, ends with Additional Discussion Questions, and is interspersed with Wired Ideas. The Wired Connections are stories that illustrate the chapter's theme, and Wired Ideas give suggestions for activities you can do with your students.

INTRO TO THE WIRED LEADER'S GUIDE

If you are an errant electrician that somehow wandered into a bookstore during your lunch break and bought this book thinking you could learn a few things about your trade, please know that you are welcome to continue to read, but this is not a journey through the intricacies of copper versus aluminum, residential or commercial, or fire hazards. Ty Pennington did not write the foreword, and Sears is not an official sponsor. Furthermore, these pages do not explore what happens when a teenager gets a dozen Krispy Kreme doughnuts and a two-liter of Red Bull in their system. That would be fun to watch, but it is not the focus of our time together.

I am going to make the educated guess that, if you are reading this book, you either have or desire some sort of influence in the lives of teenagers. There could be no greater design for your life. Whether a parent, coach, professional Christian (minister), small group leader, or volunteer at your church, pouring your life into the life of a teenager is not a random act of kindness. No, the stakes are much higher than that.

We could exhaust a million miles and hours investing a ton of very important things into the lives of students. There is so much that life experience tells us they need to know. Their needs are great. Their potential is even greater. The collective body of believers known as the church has spent an enormous amount of time as of late exploring what it means to live a life of purpose. What is interesting about this fascination with seemingly new and untold information is that there has been, since the beginning of humanity, an intrinsic, built-in desire to do one thing, and to do it and very well. It is the purpose of this book. It is the reason why we think your influence in the life of a teenager in this matter is not just important: It is critical to their life and future.

Every teenager you will ever meet has been wired to worship.

You may wrestle with such a truth. In fact, at first glance, it could be said that the last thing a teenager has been "wired" to do is worship. Wired for the opposite sex, for sure. Foolish choices, most definitely. Selfishness, a given. But worship?

Yes. Worship. Every day. All day. In every place. It's what students do. It's who teenagers are. It's what you do. It's who you are.

I received this e-mail from a high school senior recently, and I believe it expresses why the message of WIRED is so urgent and timely:

> I am a high school senior in the Atlanta area. I have been attending a traditional Methodist church for the vast majority of my life, but I have been recently intrigued by the personal stories of friends and family who have discovered alternative and more contemporary means of worship. I only recently attended my first nontraditional worship service at a church near my house, and I was amazed by how modernized and relevant the service was. The whole notion of expressing one's faith in a "contemporary" manner fascinates me, and I am in the process of conducting an investigation to go along with my own personal faith narrative. I wish to explore how contemporary worship has grown in recent decades, and I was hoping someone involved in the church and possibly rooted in its founding and principles would be willing to speak with me.

"The whole notion of expressing one's faith in a 'contemporary' manner fascinates me." Keep in mind: This is a high school SENIOR. He attends one of Atlanta's premier prep schools. What I took away from his comments was not a type of music preference or church philosophy. It was not an awakening to new and progressive worship styles. No, it was the fact that for eighteen years of his life no one has helped him understand what worship was really about. His idea of worship has been reduced to a place, a way, a song. His definition of "contemporary" has been reduced to a cool, relevant church and not his own life.

His fascination has been wired in him since his first breath.

It only makes sense that, if we have accepted the mantle of influence in a teenager's life, we steer them toward those things, that thing, that matters most. What unfolds in these pages is what we believe matters most. We are so excited that you have chosen to journey with teenagers toward this end. Hopefully and prayerfully, you will find the book you hold to be an inspiring yet practical guide to understanding this end. Here is how it works…

Your students are holding in their hands the student version of WIRED. When you flip your leader's version and their student versions over, both will take you on a 30-Day Worship Journey that we will delve into in the coming weeks. But while your version contains all the content of the student version, we have "hot-wired" the Leader's Guide to help you lead your students on an experiential journey.

Each chapter will begin with some sort of illustration or principle that will help you set your mind and heart on course. Within each chapter, there are illustrations and interactive projects to help the students you lead remember, understand, and apply what they are encountering in these pages. At the end of each chapter we have added a few additional questions. These are not for you to follow as a script, but rather a "switch" for you to turn on so that you and your teenager(s) can talk more about the content of the chapter. Students want and need to have their voices heard. These questions are intended to help you allow students to share what they are thinking about and wrestling with.

WIRED is not just anything for students. It is everything they are about. It is exactly what makes them tick, dream, and live. And it is precisely God's heart for their life.

I am praying that the weeks to follow will be a watershed time for you as an individual and as a leader of students. I am praying for the students you influence as well.

May they begin to live for His renown and fame.

Because they are wired for that life.

—Stuart

Because they are Wired for that life.

WELCOME TO **WIRED**

YOU ARE UNIQUE. In fact, as amazing as it sounds, no two of you who are holding this book in your hands are the same. You all come from various places and have different backgrounds. Each of us excels at different things, with goals and dreams that are distinct from the other. To put it another way, all of us are *wired* differently. Some are athletes, others brilliant musicians. Some are shy while others seem to be the life of the party. Some love the arts while others don't have a creative bone in their bodies. That's because God has designed each one of us in a specific way to play a unique role in His unending story. Finding our "groove" and discovering our God-given gifts and abilities is one of the most satisfying things that will ever happen to us.

But though we are all different, one thing about us is the same. While we all have varying gifts, our purpose in life is the same. In other words, we have all been prewired by God to do one thing—and to do it with everything we've got!

That's what this book is all about: discovering the central purpose of our days on earth and learning to do well what God has created us to do. And what is it? I believe we have been wired from the start to live lives of worship, lives that are billboards for the greatness and glory of God.

Hopefully, by the time you finish these pages you'll agree, and see how your life fits in God's epic adventure.

But before we get too far we need to make a deal, OK? For this journey to work it has to be a two-way street. It has to be interactive. In other words you can't just read the words on the pages, you have to jump in and get involved. There will be Scripture verses to dig into, questions to answer, and plenty of room for you to write what you're thinking.

Are you up for it? Cool. Here's the first thing.

When I say worship, what comes to your mind? What image, thought, experience, place, or definition do you see when you think of worship? Give it a little thought, and in the space below write down *your* definition of worship. Don't worry about trying to make it perfect; you're going to have a couple of opportunities to change it as we go along. Just write in your own words what you think worship is all about.

[

]

Now that you've got your worship definition going, let's look at a passage from God's Word that shines more light on the subject. Notice the verse below. What I want you to try is the "Circle the Word" Bible study method. *The what Bible study?"* Yeah, I made the name up. But the main idea is that you read the verse a few times, let its meaning and truth sink into your heart, and then circle the one or two words in the verse that seem to jump out and grab you. What words seem to mean the most to you? Sure, they are all important, but which ones are calling your name? When you know what they are (it may be just one main word), circle that word and in the space below write a few sentences about why you made that choice. Remember, there isn't a "mystery word" in the verse that gets you more credit than another. Go with the word(s) that connect with you.

(Circle the word that stands out/means most to you and be ready to talk about why you chose that word.)

Through Jesus, therefore, let us continually offer to God a sacrifice of praise—the fruit of lips that confess his name. And do not forget to do good and to share with others, for with such sacrifices God is pleased. HEBREWS 13:15–16, NIV

[   ]

All right. Now that you've got your worship definition and your first "Circle the Word" Bible study finished, you're ready to jump in. Enjoy the ride as you discover the main thing you are wired to do.

CHAPTER 1: THAT THING WE DO

When Michelangelo first saw the Pantheon in the early 1500s, he proclaimed it of "angelic and not human design." Surprisingly, at that point, this classic Roman temple, converted into a Christian church, was already more than 1350 years old. What's even more surprising is that the Pantheon, in the splendor Michelangelo admired, still stands today—another five hundred years after he saw it.

Most historians claim that Emperor Marcus Vipsanius Agrippa built the first Pantheon in 27 BC. It burned in the great fire of 80 AD, was rebuilt by Emperor Domitian, but was struck by lightning and burned again in 110 AD.

Seven years later, Hadrian, the adopted son and successor of Emperor Trajan, became Rome's ruler. Hadrian had an avid interest in Hellenic culture, especially literature, music, and architecture—so much so that his contemporaries snidely called him "the Greekling."

By 120 AD, Hadrian began designing a Pantheon reminiscent of Greek temples and far more elaborate than anything Rome had yet seen. The rotunda's internal geometry creates a perfect sphere, since the height of the rotunda to the top of its dome matches its diameter: 142 feet (43.3 meters). At its top, the dome has an oculus, or eye, a circular opening with a diameter of 27 feet (8.2 meters), which is its only light source. Hadrian visualized himself enthroned directly under the Pantheon's oculus—a near deity around whom the Roman Empire and also the universe, the sun, and the heavens obediently revolved.

Hadrian's engineers dug a circular trench 26 feet (8 meters) wide and 15 feet (4.5 meters) deep for the rotunda's foundation and rectangular trenches for the pronaos and the connector. They lined the trenches with timber forms and layered those with pozzolana cement—powerful cement that the Romans discovered they could make by grinding together lime and a volcanic product found at Pozzuoli, Italy.

Eventually, work began on the concrete dome, constructed in tapering courses or steps that are thickest at the base (20 feet) and thinnest at the oculus (7.5 feet). The Romans used the heaviest aggregate, mostly basalt, at the bottom and lighter materials, such as pumice or volcanic ash, at the top. They embedded empty clay jugs into the dome's upper courses to further lighten the structure and facilitate the concrete's curing.

The Pantheon is the only structure of its age, size, and span that has successfully survived the scourge of time and gravity and has come down to us intact and in all its splendor and beauty.[i]

Who cares? What is the point?

It was not until 1818, some 2,000 years later, that natural cement was produced in the United States.

Isn't it amazing how unique we think things are to us? You haven't thought about this because you think it is unique to you and simply normal. America (or any other country for that matter) did not discover concrete for some 2,000-plus years, yet the Romans built 5,000 miles of roads and scores of buildings with it.

We think we can trump principles and patterns that have been true since the Bible was being lived out. The truth that you are wired to worship is one such truth…

What other youth workers are saying about worship:*

—*Worship is our response to, and magnification of, God.*

—*Worship is pleasing God always.*

* Gathered from youth workers at Louie's breakout session at The Purpose Driven Youth Ministry Conference, spring 2005.

THAT THING WE DO

THE HUGE IDEA:

EVERYBODY WORSHIPS SOMETHING.

You, my friend...are a worshiper!

There, I said it.

Every day, all day long, everywhere you go, you worship. It's what you do. It's who you are.

So if by chance you have only a few seconds to check out this book, that's what it's all about. We all are worshipers, created to bring pleasure and glory to the God who made us.

I don't know whether or not you consider yourself a "worshiping" kind of person, but you cannot help but worship—something.

It's what you were made to do.

Should you for some reason choose not to give God what He desires, you'll still worship something—exchanging the Creator for something He has created.

>> Whatever's Worth Most

Think of it this way: Worship is simply about value. The simplest definition I can give is this: Worship is our response to what we value most.

That's why worship is that thing we all do. It's

THE HUGE IDEA:

EVERYBODY WORSHIPS

SOMETHING.

what we're all about on any given day. Because worship is about saying, "This person, this thing, this experience (this whatever) is what matters most to me…it's the thing I put first in my life."

That "thing" might be a relationship. A dream. Friends. Status. Stuff. A name. Some kind of pleasure. Whatever name you put on it, this thing or person is what you've concluded in your heart is worth most to you. And whatever is worth most to you is—you guessed it—what you worship.

Worship tells us what we value most. As a result, worship determines our actions, becoming the driving force for all we do.

And we're not just talking about the religious crowd. Christians. The churchgoer among us. Or the youth group attender. We're talking about everybody on planet earth…a multitude of souls proclaiming with every breath what is worthy of their affection, their attention, their allegiance. Proclaiming with every step what it is they worship.

Some of us attend the church on the corner, professing to worship the Living God above all. Others who rarely step inside the church doors

Worship is our **response** to what we **value** most.

would say worship isn't a part of their lives because they aren't "religious." But everybody has an altar. And every altar has a throne.

So how do you know where and what you worship?

It's easy. You simply follow the trail of your time, your affection, your energy, your money, and your loyalty. At the end of that trail you'll find a throne; and whatever, or whomever, is on that throne is what's of highest value to you. On that throne is what you worship.

Sure, not too many of us walk around saying, "I worship my stuff. I worship my Xbox. I worship this pleasure. I worship her. I worship my body. I worship me!"

But the trail never lies. We may say we value this thing or that thing more than any other, but the volume of our actions speaks louder than our words.

In the end, our worship is more about what we do than what we say.

WIRED Idea: Have students bring their schedules, credit card or bank statements, and cell phone bills. (We are not advocating the teen cell phone rage, but if they have them, let's use them as an illustration.) If a student does not have these things, have them write down a typical schedule and estimate how much money they spend per month and on what they spend it. Use these as an illustration of a trail that leads to what a student values most.

One interesting point to make: Many Christian students will talk of how much they love God. But when you examine the practical areas of their lives, there is little evidence of such allegiance. This is a powerful way to illustrate this point.

Worship is *the* activity of the human **soul**.

>> Everywhere—Worship

Worship is *the* activity of the human soul.

So not only do all people worship, but they worship all the time. Worship isn't just a Sunday thing. It's an all-the-time thing.

Right now, all around you, people of all shapes and sizes, people of every age and purpose are worshiping—continually making decisions based on what they value most. Worship happens everywhere…all day long.

In fact, some of the purest forms of worship are found outside the walls of the church and have no reference to the God of all creation. All you have to do is drop in on a concert at the local arena or go to a sporting event at a nearby stadium to see amazing worship. People are going for it, lifting their hands, shouting like crazy, staking their claim, standing in awe, declaring their allegiance. Interestingly, these venues are filled with the same forms of worship mentioned in the pages of God's Word—the same expressions of worship that God desires and deserves.

A while back, watching an interview Oprah was doing with Michael Jackson in the prime of his career, I was stunned with the reality of this truth. What I witnessed as she showed a video clip of people responding to him in concert settings around the world absolutely floored me. Talk about amazing worship!

In multiple cultures, mobs of people numbering into the hundreds of thousands were glued as one to his every move. On every continent they gathered like an army, waving their hands in the air. Some fell to their knees. Others strained with outstretched hands, hoping for a brief touch from his. Seared in my mind is the image of one young girl with a look on her face of total awe.

I couldn't believe it. What I was watching was some of the most intense worship I'd ever seen… anywhere. Far more "full-on" than much of what I'd experienced inside the church.

And for what? Granted, Michael Jackson is a living legend when it comes to entertainment, but he's not a great god. Not even close. Yet the worship was phenomenal, demonstrating the God-given capacity for adoration that is rooted in the soul of every man.

What do you see people around you worshiping most?

Think about the last concert or sporting event you attended. Write down some of the ways you saw people responding to the game/musicians. Did you see worship happening? If so, how?

And you can see it when your favorite band plays, or your favorite team. People naturally doing the thing it seems we were all created to do.

>> Connectivity, Prewired

In the same way, we all (you and me) worship something all the time. And you know what? We're really good at it.

If you think about it, history has known no shortage of worship. The timeline of mankind is littered with trillions of little idols. Every culture, every corner of earth, every age has had its gods. Just circle the globe and watch for worship. Study the great civilizations and explore their temples.

The compelling question for me is, "Why?" Why do we crave something to worship? Why are we so insatiably drawn from idol to idol, desperately in need of something to champion, something to exalt, something to adore?

How do we know for sure that some things are more important than others, more worthy of worship? How do we even know that value, beauty, and worth exist?

WIRED Idea: With their parents' consent, attend a sporting event or music concert (Christian or secular) with your students. Consider the following questions and perspectives as you enjoy the event:

- What is the reaction of the fans that attend a sporting event or concert?
- How much influence does a team or artist have over the audience?
- What specifically did you notice about the way people responded to certain songs or the team or artist themselves?
- Do you think you experienced worship?
- Why is music such a powerful force?

I think it's because we were designed that way. We were made *for* God.

The Bible says it this way: All things were made *by* Him; and all things were made *for* Him (Colossians 1:16).

You've been created by God. And if that wasn't enough, you've also been created *for* Him. As a result, there's an internal homing device riveted deep within your soul that perpetually longs for your Maker. An internal, Godward magnet, pulling your being toward Him.

Stamped in God's image, we know that there's something we attach to, something we fit with, someone we belong to, somewhere called home.

That's why we come from the womb equipped for connectivity with God, prewired to praise. And that's why, from the youngest age, we begin to worship.

WIRED Idea: Use a mirror to illustrate the idea of "mirrored souls designed to reflect His glory." Hold a bathroom-sized (three feet by four feet) mirror against your body and talk about how just as people see a reflection of something from the mirror, others see a reflection of something from our lives. Maybe it is popularity. The opposite sex. Power. Greed. But we reflect something. We were created to reflect God not only to the world but, most importantly, to God. This is what Paul means when he writes in Colossians 1:16 that "by him all things were created: things in heaven and on earth, visible and invisible, whether thrones or powers or rulers or authorities; all things were created by him and for him" (NIV).

What makes our reason for existence so difficult is that sin has "shattered" our mirrored soul. We were born with a nature that is sinful. If you want, place your mirror on an easel and break the mirror with a rock or baseball. (To diminish the mess, you may want to gaff tape the back of the mirror and lay a sheet out under the easel.) This illustrates the effect of sin on our souls and the difficulty we have reflecting a pure and whole picture of God back to God and to the world.

CIRCLE THE WORD BIBLE STUDY

(Circle the word that stands out/means most to you and be ready to talk about why you chose that word.)

[Jesus] is the image of the invisible God, the firstborn over all creation. For by him all things were created: things in heaven and on earth, visible and invisible, whether thrones or powers or rulers or authorities; all things were created by him and for him. He is before all things, and in him all things hold together.

COLOSSIANS 1:15-17, NIV

We arrive in this world as objects of divine affection, miraculous receptors designed to bring Him pleasure. If only everyone could *know* we've been created by and for God! If only we could all comprehend that we're precious to Him, housing mirrored souls designed to reflect His glory.

>> The Question That Captivates Us All

As I'm writing, my flight home to Atlanta is climbing high above the Chicago night. Staring out across the horizon, I'm captivated by the thousands of tiny lights dotting the landscape as far as I can see. Countless twinkling stars of earth, hundreds of thousands of beacon lights. It's like a sea of little lights—streetlights, headlights, house lights, neon lights…all kinds of lights.

And I'm thinking, everywhere I see lights, there are people. People everywhere. A sea of humanity. And every single person down there is someone created with amazing potential and purpose. All uniquely fashioned to reflect back to their Creator His beauty and wonder. Each one breathing the air of earth in one accord. Each person given life to give Him praise.

And that's only the view in one direction, looking out over just one city, in just one state, in one nation, on one continent.

I'm floored. As we jet through the darkened sky, I think of how this earth is home to billions of worshipers, created to light the darkness with stories of who God is…with echoes of all He has done.

But do they know it? Do *you* know it? Do you know in this moment that you were made by and for God?

While we soar over Chicago, our plane is just a little tiny speck to anyone who might look up and see us, a little dot of light blinking its way through the night. Yet on board this night are even more people. People everywhere.

Across the aisle from me, a middle-aged woman is digging into a well-worn Bible. (No, I'm not making this up!) She's leaning forward as she reads, as if she knows this Book holds some secret key. I'm thinking how the same God who's worthy of all the earth's worship is the Author of the very pages in her hands. She's holding His autobiography in her hands. There before her eyes is the extension of God's hand. And she's devouring it in large chunks, miraculously forgoing another showing of *My Big Fat Greek Wedding*. It's as if somehow within its pages she has discovered life's very meaning.

It seems we all are eventually captivated by the question of why. Why are we here? Is there a reason for our lives? Is there something we're uniquely destined to do?

It's the age-old dilemma—what's the purpose of life?

The answer begins and ends with God. Simply put, you and I were made by Him and made for Him. You and I exist for one purpose alone—to reflect back to God His matchless glory. You were made for a unique relationship with Him. And your life was designed to be a mirror that reflects all the best things about Him to the world around you. Finding our Maker and connecting with His purposes is the one thing we are all seeking.

Okay, to be fair, things have change on board. Forty minutes have passed, and the woman across the aisle is now reading a David Baldacci novel, sending occasional glances toward the movie monitor.

Uh-oh. The headphones are going on. I think she's being sucked into the movie.

Apparently, she's seen *My Big Fat Greek Wedding* a dozen times and is having no difficulty jumping right into the flow. It hasn't been thirty seconds and she's already laughing. (Not as loudly as the guy in front of me, mind you, who with headphones on is loudly giving a blow-by-blow commentary of each scene to the stranger trapped beside him.)

I guess tonight won't see a miracle after all. The

This first chapter defines worship as "our response to what we value most" and "declaring what we value most." Is this a new or larger way of looking at worship for you? In what ways does it make you question or rethink the way you've viewed worship before?

"little movie engine that could" wins again. The unstoppable force of "Big Fat Greek Wedding" rambles on. But she still gets major credit for her deep dive into the pages of God's Word. For she—just like the rest of us—is seeking God. And, as far as I can tell, finding Him on a plane to Georgia.

(The guy next to me is sound asleep. The lady in front is talking in what sounds like a South African accent. The flight attendant buzzing around is tall and Romanian. A businessman behind me is wide-awake and feverishly working.)

And there are people all around you, too. Today as you stretch before practice, sit at the picnic table during lunch, or study in the library, there are people everywhere. Over there the little popular clump of girls who think they rule the world. Then there's that quiet, shy kid who always seems to sit alone. And near him two teachers deep in conversation who seem to have tuned out the entire school.

All these people.

Do they know their lives have an amazing purpose?

Do you?

ADDITIONAL DISCUSSION QUESTIONS

CHAPTER 1: THAT THING WE DO

1. This chapter asserts that all of us are always worshiping. How have you recognized this to be true in your life or the lives of those around you? Can you see it in your choices and actions over the past twenty-four hours?

2. How can we go about deciding—in an honest and thorough way—what it is we value most in life? How do we effectively and accurately "follow the trail" in order to evaluate how we spend our time? Our affection? Our energy? Our money? Our allegiance?

3. Here are some Scripture passages to explore and discuss together: Colossians 1:15–17; John 1:1–3; 1 Corinthians 8:5–6.

CHAPTER 2: SOMETHING MORE

In the September 20, 2005 issue of Astrophysical Journal, an article about new observations by astronomers reports that astronomers using the Hubble Space Telescope have identified the source of a mysterious blue light surrounding a supermassive black hole in our neighboring galaxy of Andromeda.

This "mysterious blue light" has puzzled astronomers since it was first spotted a decade ago. Astronomers have determined that this light is coming from a disk of hot, young stars that are whipping around the black hole in much the same way planets in our solar system revolve around the sun.

Interestingly enough, this finding raises new questions because the black hole's intense gravitational force should have torn apart any matter long before it could coalesce to form new stars. In other words, science does not explain how this can happen.[ii]

Maybe it is because there is something more…

What other youth workers are saying about worship:

—*Worship is a life where God is at the center of all we do.*

—*Worship is being alive for Christ.*

SOMETHING MORE

THE HUGE IDEA:

WE ARE MADE TO WORSHIP GOD.

EVERYBODY WORSHIPS SOMETHING.

I think people know there's something more to life,

though I have no clue if they know who *He* is.

A quick glance at history tells me we have always been searching for something.

In the New Testament book of Acts (a historical overview of the expansion of the early Christian church) we find the main character, Paul, entering Athens to proclaim the gospel. Right smack in the middle of the intellectual center of the known world, Paul found Athens to be a "city full of idols."

In fact, he found a multitude of idols to gods of every name and description. But one idol seized his heart, quickly becoming the focus of his message to the Athenian people. The inscription on this altar read, "TO AN UNKNOWN GOD."

Even with all their idols and altars, these intellectual and cultural giants wanted to cover their bases, making sure all deities were happy in the event there was something, or someone, more. The altar "UNKNOWN" stood among them, just in case it turned out that another object of worship was superior to all the others.

THE HUGE IDEA:

WE ARE MADE

TO WORSHIP GOD.

What are some ways that history proves to us that man has always been searching for God?

Intrigued by Paul's teaching, the council of moral overseers known as the Areopagus invited him to speak to their assembly. It didn't take Paul long to get to the point.

"Men of Athens," he began, crafting a simple and straight-to-the-heart response, "I see that you are religious in every respect. For passing through your objects of worship I also found an altar with this inscription, 'TO AN UNKNOWN GOD.' What you worship in ignorance, I proclaim to you" (17:22-23).

Paul didn't find a lack of worship in Athens. In fact, there was no apathy in their worship. Just uncertainty. Worshiping people wondering if there was something more.

A lot has changed since Athens of old. Its ancient idols and altars lie in ruins. But students everywhere are still searching…still building altars to everything under the sun. Wondering if there's a God they can know.

>> Ultimate Search

God is always seeking you. Every sunset. Every clear blue sky. Every ocean wave. The starry host of night. He blankets each new day with the invitation, "I am here."

It's a kind of revelation that is accessible to all—God constantly exposing His creative power to anyone watching. Add to that the internal magnet we've already talked about, and you understand what it means when His Word says God has placed eternity in our hearts (Ecclesiastes 3:11).

Somehow, we know He's there. The creation surrounding us tells us there's more to this life than living and dying.

Yet painted skies and a spinning earth aren't enough to tell His story. Heaven's hosts and atom's wonder are a revelation still incomplete. God's face couldn't be clearly known...until His Son appeared—God on the ultimate search, appearing in human flesh. God coming down to restore and redeem fallen man.

To us, ready or not, Jesus came. To us, worthy or not, He appeared. Accepting or not, we find His footprints in Palestinian soil.

It's history. It's fact. It's inescapable. Jesus came. And in His own words, He came to "seek and to save that which was lost" (Luke 19:10).

God wants you to know Him.

Searching for Him isn't like looking for a needle in a theological haystack. He isn't hiding. He isn't unknowable. He isn't some mysterious force or philosophical construct that you can't quite grasp or attain.

In fact, the opposite is true. His Son appeared to all in bodily form. Jesus, "the radiance of God's glory and the exact representation of his being" (Hebrews 1:3, NIV), walked this earth in plain sight so that anyone seeking God could find their way to Him.

God's not hiding. He's been looking for you for a long, long time.

Do you know why? Because He wants you to know who He is…and who you are, too. He wants you to know that you're the object of His affection, created in His image, made by and for Him.

He wants you to know that the Unknown God has a name. He wants you to know that the incredible desire for worship rooted deep inside your heart was crafted for Him.

God wants
you to know Him.

CIRCLE THE WORD BIBLE STUDY

(Circle the word that stands out/means most to you and be ready to talk about why you chose that word.)

The God who made the world and all things in it, since He is the Lord of heaven and earth, does not dwell in temples made with hands; nor is He served by human hands, as though He needed anything, since He Himself gives to all *people* life and breath and all things. Acts 17:24-25

>> Meet God

Standing before the men of Athens, Paul took a deep breath and unfolded the mystery that his listeners had been searching for. He spoke of "the God who made the world and all things in it." Paul identified Him as "Lord of heaven and earth." And this God, Paul said, "gives to all people life and breath and all things."

Men of Athens, meet the God of gods.

Turns out they were right all along. There *was* another God greater than all their idols, higher than all the objects inhabiting their altars.

This God is powerful enough, Paul proclaimed, to invent the whole world and everything it contains. And He "does not dwell in temples made with hands, nor is He served by human hands, as though He needed anything." Turns out, God doesn't live at the church after all. By the very logic of His immensity, He refuses to be contained by any church or structure.

What a shame. I guess we have to say good-bye to the warning we all were threatened with as kids, *"SHHHhhhh! You're in God's house!"* Although I have to admit it did strike the fear of God into me as I considered that the church building was actually *where* He lived.

It does make for a nice image, though. Can you see Him at the door after the service, greeting everyone? "Thanks for coming, appreciate you being here, glad you made it, hope you enjoyed it. Was everything okay? God bless. Oh yeah, *I'm* God—so, just…bless! Come back to see Me! Have a nice week!"

Is that God? Watching all the cars drive away, turning the church lights off, settling in for a long and quiet week, maybe playing a little on the organ, only to fling wide the doors again in seven days. "Hey! Glad you're back. Good to see you. Come on in!"

I don't think so. God isn't stuck in church-world. He might even care less about us running in the church halls than we think! Why? Because He's huge. Creator. Initiator of all things. Way too vast to be stuck in some building all week. Far too interested in our lives to simply watch us drive away from Him. Much more worthy of our time than just one hour of just one day.

This God is all-sufficient God. He doesn't need a thing! He made the world and everything in it. Paul wanted the men of Athens to know that He's the constant supply of life, breath—everything!

And he wanted them to know that God is near.

>> Near...Now

God is really close to you in this very moment. Right now, He's near. You may not feel it, or sense it, but it's true.

Paul kept describing this huge and limitless God. He said God has "determined" for all human beings "their appointed times [the span of our lives] and the boundaries of their habitation [the details of our existence]…"(Acts 17:26).

WIRED Idea: Ask students to list what they think about when they think about the word "church." Where were most of these ideas of church formulated? What ideas are correct? What ideas are warped?

In what ways in your life have you seen that God has been searching for you? How have you noticed His "internal magnet" at work inside you? How have you been aware that He's placed eternity in your heart?

And all for what purpose? Check it out: "…that men [all people] would seek him and perhaps reach out for him and find him, though he is not far from each one of us. For in him we live and move and have our being" (v. 28, NIV).

No wonder the whole world is filled with worshipers. Every last one of us has been created with a searching soul, designed that way by God so we would find no rest until we find our rest in Him.

If you've been wrestling with big questions of ultimate truth, don't be alarmed. If you feel at times like you're inching your way through a murky night in search of home, you're not alone. The journey to God isn't like hopscotch on a chalk-lined sidewalk. It's more like a continual reaching for someone our eyes cannot see.

That's why it's comforting to know God is seeking you, too.

He's seeking you so you can know just how amazing He is. He's seeking you so you can know what you're created to do. He's seeking you so you can find Him and value Him with all your heart.

He's seeking you because He's God…and He knows you can't live without Him.

That, my friend, explains a ton of stuff for us.

For one, it explains why you worship and why you're so good at it. It's why the whole world is worshiping in this moment. And it explains why Jesus willingly came. He came to connect us to God and awaken us to the possibility of centering our worship on who and what matters most…forever.

ADDITIONAL DISCUSSION QUESTIONS

CHAPTER 2: SOMETHING MORE

1. Are you fully convinced that God wants you to know who He is and what He's like? Why or why not?

3. In what times of your life have you wrestled most with questions of "ultimate truth"?

4. Talk about the ways in which you identify with the following statement from this chapter: "The journey to God isn't like hopscotch on a chalk-lined sidewalk. It's more like a continual reaching for someone our eyes cannot see."

5. Think about all that Paul told the Athenians. Which parts of his message to them are most meaningful to you, and why?

6. Some words from God to explore together: Ecclesiastes 3:11; Hebrews 1:1–3; Acts 17:15–34.

WIRED CONNECTION

CHAPTER 3: WHY WORSHIP MATTERS

This would be a great exercise to do with your students...

Open your daily paper's sports pages to the box scores. You might want to pause and ask yourself why your hometown paper devotes an entire section to sports. The implication is that the readers' need to know the outcome of sporting contests ranks up there in importance with their need to know about global politics, business, and the arts. Compare that with the amount of column inches per week on religion; it's not even close.

For each box score, consider how many moods hung in the balance over the game's outcome. Maybe tens of thousands attended in person. They may have "gone wild," or "gone crazy," telling clichés we use to describe the behavior of fans. Thousands more—millions more if we're talking about a big play-off game in some sports—watched at home or listened on their car radios. If it was a close game, it's possible that some of those people had the most intense emotional experiences of their lives, more acute than anything they'd felt at home with their spouses or kids. If this sounds like hyperbole, think of the most emotionally intense moments in your own life—when you realized you were in love, when your child was born, or when someone you cared for accomplished something important, like graduating from college. You were profoundly happy, but you probably didn't hug the stranger next to you. Most likely, you didn't "go wild." You probably didn't tear down a goalpost.

Now look at the all the other box scores in the sports pages and consider how many hundreds of thousands of Americans were on similar trips last night. Think about all the newspapers published in the world today, all their sports pages and box scores. Now think, if you can grasp it, of all the people in the world last night who watched sports. America has football, baseball, and men's and women's basketball. Europe, South America, Africa, and parts of the Middle East have soccer. Canada and Russia have hockey. The Japanese like baseball, too, and also sumo wrestling; Pakistanis, squash and cricket. Car racing is popular the world over.

In Afghanistan there is a traditional game that involves two teams fighting on horseback for control of a ram's carcass. There's probably some kind of box score for that (Cowboys 10, Rams nothing?). It's dizzying, especially when you realize what you just got your head around was one day's worth of sports in the world, and that the cycle will repeat itself this evening. Millions more moods will hang in the balance, and the papers tomorrow will be full of another round of box scores. And so on, like the tides.[iii]

Be very careful of what you value most....

What other youth workers are saying about **worship**:

—Worship is living a life that is part of God's story.

—Worship is living your life in such a way that you are always aware of the presence of God and always seeking to give glory to Him.

WHY WORSHIP MATTERS

THE HUGE IDEA:

WE NEED TO WORSHIP GOD MORE THAN GOD NEEDS OUR WORSHIP.

WE ARE MADE TO WORSHIP GOD.

EVERYBODY WORSHIPS SOMETHING.

When the subject is worship, the stakes are high—

because worship is what God is all about.

Worship should matter to you simply because it matters to God. And worship matters to God because He knows He's worthy. I know that doesn't sound too persuasive in our me-centered culture, but it's true. Worship doesn't begin with us. Worship begins and ends with God. And God is worthy of all praise, from all people, for all time.

God is the center of everything that exists. Above all the little gods of earth, He alone is the Creator. Sustainer. Originator. Life Giver. Beauty Maker.

That's why every glimpse into God's presence throughout the pages of His Word affirms that God dwells in endless praise.

Notice the angel host of Revelation, never ceasing to say, "Holy, holy, holy is the Lord God, the Almighty, who was and who is and who is to come" (Revelation 4:8). Never do they stop. Day and night they proclaim. Always affirming His infinite worth.

And "the heavens are telling of the glory of God; and their expanse is declaring the work of His

Worship begins and ends with God.

THE HUGE IDEA:

WE NEED TO WORSHIP GOD MORE THAN GOD NEEDS OUR WORSHIP.

hands" (Psalm 19:1). Why? Because that's what they were created to do, day after day—to tell God (and anyone else who's paying attention) that He is huge. All-powerful. Glorious. Limitless. Beyond our wildest imagination.

And you know what's really wild? This massive God, who has never known any shortage of worship, wants to be worshiped…*by you*. Right now.

It's not that He needs any more worship to be worthy. No, God can't be more worthy than He already is and always has been. It's not that God needs our worship—but that He wants it. He wants it because He deserves it. And He commands it because to do so is the most loving thing He can possibly do.

God knows who He is. He knows what He's worth. And He knows the best thing He can give us is Himself.

CIRCLE THE WORD BIBLE STUDY

(Circle the word that stands out/means most to you and be ready to talk about why you chose that word.)

"To whom will you compare me? Or who is my equal?" says the Holy One. Lift your eyes and look to the heavens: Who created all of these? He who brings out the starry host one by one, and calls them each by name. Because of His great power and mighty strength, not one of them is missing. ISAIAH 40:25-26, NIV

>> Don't Waste Your Worship

Worship should matter to you because you are and always will be a worshiper. It's what you do. You can't help it. You can't stop it. You can't live without it. But you can choose where you invest it. You can choose to make your worship count for today and for eternity.

We're created to worship. That's why you and I are going to spend our lives declaring the worth of something. As a result, we've got to make sure the thing we declare to be of greatest value is really worthy in the long run.

For me, I've got to keep making sure that what matters most—matters most to me.

The same is true of you. It's imperative that you find an object worthy of your affection. It's essential that you find a God worthy of your life's devotion.

You only have one life. And you only have one life of worship. You have one brief opportunity in time to declare your allegiance, to unleash your affection, to exalt something or someone above all else.

Don't waste your worship on some little god, squandering your birthright on idols made only

WIRED Idea: Have students seriously work through the following list of possible gods and their worthiness for affection: On a scale of one to ten (one being most, ten being least), how would you rank the worthiness of each of these as it relates to your affections and attention:

Partying • Sports • School • Friends • Cars • Clothes • Popularity • Money

One thing to remember: If there is no God and life ends when you die, then your ranking might be different. But life does not end when you die. And that changes everything.

with human imagination. Guard your worship…
and carefully evaluate all potential takers.

To choose well doesn't mean that we can't
appreciate things of beauty and style. It's certainly
not wrong to deeply love another. Nor is it a sin to
really be into playing soccer or to get stoked over a
trip to your favorite destination.

But when we elevate any of these things to the
highest place in our hearts, we've gone too far.

For great is the Lord and most worthy of praise.
He is to be feared above all gods. For all the gods of
the nations are idols, but the Lord made the heavens. Splendor and majesty are before Him; strength
and glory are in His sanctuary.

>> The War for Your Worship

Worship also matters because every day there's a
battle for your worship.

The things we elevate—the values we serve—
none of those choices are made in a vacuum.

CIRCLE THE WORD BIBLE STUDY

(Circle the word that stands out/means most to you and be ready to talk about why you chose that word.)

For great is the LORD, and most worthy of praise; he is to be feared above all

gods. For all the gods of the nations are idols, but the LORD made the heavens.

PSALM 96:4-5, NIV

Worship also matters because **every day** there's a **battle** for your **worship**.

There's a war raging for our worship, and it's been raging since before there was time.

Even before the earth was formed, one of God's highest angels bolted from His presence, refusing to join the ranks of the true worshipers, refusing to exalt God above all. The account records that in a flash Satan fell like lightning from heaven. Exalting himself more than God, Satan was banned from His presence (Luke 10:18).

Yet, having been in God's presence, Satan knows God is central and worthy of all praise. He's heard the anthem. He's seen the glory.

But because of pride, he couldn't bow. Spurred on by self, he leads a band of fallen brothers, spreading his mutiny to as many as he can.

That's where we come in.

How does Satan advance his rebellion against God today? By contesting His supremacy throughout the earth, leading a traitor race to exchange "the truth of God for a lie," and to worship and serve "the creature rather than the Creator, who is blessed forever" (Romans 1:25). Satan can't stop worship from happening, but he'll deceive anyone who lets him, leading them to empty wells and puny gods.

Let's check back in with Paul. Remember his message to the men of Athens? Remember his audience? The council Paul addressed that day was called the Areopagus, named after Ares, the Greek god of war. Isn't it interesting that this is the setting God chose for Paul to give this address on the real meaning of life? God's words of truth landed in the very arena where opinions battled.

In the same way, the very fallen angel who challenged Him will challenge what God is saying to you. That challenge is called temptation. Deception. Falsehood. Lies. Theft.

Do you know what God desires most from you? It's the one thing no other person on earth can give Him—your affection. Although a thousand other people can do the work, give the bucks, fill the gap...no one else can give God the unique affection that only you and He can share.

But just as much as God longs for your love, there's an enemy who seeks to steal it.

At this point, you may be saying, "I didn't start this war of worship—and I don't care to be in it.

Why does Satan want to
steal your worship?
What are some ways you
see that happening in
your life?

I just want to live my life, make my own choices, and do my own thing."

That, however, is not an option. Our lives are on loan from God, a sacred trust of opportunities and decisions. And every one of our choices is made on a battlefield with heavenly ramifications.

>> The Last Temptation

Even Jesus faced the same fate.

Before going public with His ministry, Jesus was led by God's Spirit into a wilderness challenge. At thirty years old, Jesus was preparing for all that was ahead by fasting for forty days and nights. He was learning how to depend on His Father, clinging to Him for life itself.

As His fast was coming to a close, Jesus was physically drained but spiritually sharp. The enemy, no doubt seeing that Jesus looked weary, closed in with three potent temptations.

You remember the first: "If You're so hungry, turn these rocks into bread."

And the second: "If You're the Son of God, leap from the height of the temple. Surely Your Father will catch You long before You hit the ground."

But notice the last temptation. With this one Satan tried to highjack Christ's worship.

The offer: all the world's kingdoms if Jesus would bow down and worship him. What on earth was Satan thinking? To ask the Son of God to bow down and worship a foolish exile of heaven, someone doomed to die, someone banished to an eternal future void of the beauty of angels' sounds—talk about being deceived!

Jesus' reply was clear. "It has already been written: Worship the Lord your God and serve Him only" (Matthew 4:1–11).

Your worship matters to God. If it didn't, Satan wouldn't care about trying to steal it from God… and from you.

>> Be Careful What You Choose

There's one more reason worship should really matter to you—whatever you worship, you become.

You can worship whatever you want, but there'll always be a last twist to the story: Whatever you worship, you become obsessed with. Whatever you become obsessed with, you imitate. And whatever you imitate, you become.

In other words, whatever you value most will ultimately determine who you are.

If you worship money, you'll become greedy at the core of your heart. If you worship some sinful habit, that same sin will grip your soul and poison your character to death. If you worship stuff, your life will become material, void of eternal significance. If you give all your praise to the god of you, you'll become a disappointing little god both to yourself and to all those who trust in you.

Listen to the psalm writer: "Not to us, O LORD, not to us but to your name be the glory, because of your love and faithfulness." Then comes this observation: "Our God is in heaven; he does whatever pleases him" (Psalm 115:1, 3, NIV).

WIRED Idea: There is a great scene in the movie *Tombstone* that illustrates the idea of becoming what you worship. It's late, and the last rays of the sun are coming through the window, falling on the bed where Doc Holliday lies, awake but looking near death. His friend Wyatt Earp sits next to him, staring at the floor. After a moment, this dialogue transpires:

WYATT: What makes a man like Ringo, Doc? What makes him do the things he does?

DOC: A man like Ringo's got a great empty hole right through the middle of him and no matter what he does he can't ever fill it. He can't kill enough or steal enough or inflict enough pain to ever fill it. And it drives him mad. Sick mad. Cold and dirty.

WYATT: So what does he want?

DOC: What does he want? He wants revenge.

WYATT: Revenge? For what?

Doc looks at him, a look of purest sadness in his sunken eyes.

DOC: Being born.

The truth is, "We become what we worship"—how have you recognized this to be true?

Then, by contrast, he describes the idols men make and choose:

> *But their idols are silver and gold,*
> *made by the hands of men. They have*
> *mouths, but cannot speak, eyes, but*
> *they cannot see; they have ears, but*
> *cannot hear, noses, but they cannot*
> *smell; they have hands, but cannot feel,*
> *feet, but they cannot walk; nor can they*
> *utter a sound with their throats.*
> (vv.4–7, NIV)

Not too high of a score for the man-made gods. But here's the clincher:

> *Those who make them will be like*
> *them, and so will all who trust in*
> *them.* (v. 8, NIV)

Simply put: We become what we worship. If you don't like who you're becoming, take a quick inventory of the things on the throne of your heart. If you want to become more and more like Jesus, keep your worship focused squarely on Him.

ADDITIONAL DISCUSSION QUESTIONS

CHAPTER 3: WHY WORSHIP MATTERS

1. Worship is what God is all about...and God is what worship is all about. Discuss what those statements mean to you, and your response to them.

2. Knowing that there's a "war" for our worship—that an enemy seeks to steal the love that God longs to receive uniquely from each one of us—how should that affect our thinking about worship and our approach to worship?

3. In what situations can you most easily recognize the battle going on for your values and for your worship?

4. We're encouraged in this chapter to "guard" our worship so that we don't squander it "on idols made only with human imagination." What are the best ways to guard our worship?

5. Scripture passages to explore and talk about together: Matthew 4:1–11; Psalm 115:1–8; Revelation 4:8.

CHAPTER 4: WHAT GOD WANTS MOST FOR YOU

Ever wondered if a spiderweb could really support the weight of a man swinging through the air? Could someone actually catch a speeding bullet? Well, yes. In *The Physics of Superheroes,* University of Minnesota professor James Kakalios examines whether Spider-Man, Superman, and other comic book characters obey real-world laws of nature.

How can Superman leap tall buildings in a single bound? Let's say a tall building is about one-eighth of a mile high—his legs must exert about 6,000 pounds of force against the ground. Superman's muscles and skeleton are adapted to Krypton's gravity, which is much stronger than Earth's. If 6,000 pounds is about twice his weight on Krypton, and he weighs about 220 pounds on Earth, then the gravity on his home planet must be roughly 15 times greater than it is on ours.

Why doesn't the Human Torch's costume burn? The Fantastic Four's jumpsuits are supposedly made of unstable molecules. But unstable molecules tend to fall apart or explode. More realistically, the Torch's outfit uses shape-memory materials that return to their original configuration after being deformed by heat, pressure, or an electrical field.

What about Nightcrawler and his teleportation abilities? There would have to be some major discovery in the laws of physics in order to teleport. But one thing that is scientifically accurate about Nightcrawler is the Bamf! sound when he teleports. Nightcrawler suddenly disappears, leaving a vacuum behind. This creates a sudden inrushing of air for a few nanoseconds, which results in a very loud noise.

How do Wonder Woman's bullet-deflecting bracelets work? Well, the cuffs themselves are made of bulletproof metal—no mystery there. But her wrists must be incredibly strong to withstand more than 70,000 pounds per square inch without snapping.[iv]

Amazing, isn't it, how much time it must have taken to figure this out, when in reality, there is a Someone who truly is supernatural and wants to rescue us from ourselves?

What other youth workers are saying about worship:

—*Worship is embracing the Father continually.*

—*Worship is acknowledging and appreciating God for His attributes, sacrifice, and love, and responding with every aspect of my life.*

WHAT GOD WANTS MOST FOR YOU

THE HUGE IDEA:

**TRUE WORSHIP BEGINS AT
THE CROSS OF CHRIST.**

WE NEED TO WORSHIP GOD MORE THAN
GOD NEEDS OUR WORSHIP.

WE ARE MADE TO WORSHIP GOD.

EVERYBODY WORSHIPS SOMETHING.

God loves you very much.

But God also loves Himself, because to do anything less would mean not being God. More than any of us, God knows how valuable He is. He knows He's God. He knows He's central. As a result, He values Himself above all things.

No, He's not egotistical, thinking more highly of Himself than He should. He's the only God, so it's imperative that He think of Himself as He truly is.

But God's centrality hasn't stopped Him from loving you with the greatest love known to man. And through the death of His Son, God has made a way for you to return to His loving arms, washed clean and forgiven because of the price He paid at the cross of Jesus Christ.

Where your spirit was once dormant because of sin (sin didn't make us bad, sin made us dead!), God seeks to stir your soul to life again, giving you the capacity to walk in intimacy with Him. Restoring your ability to worship Him with all your heart.

God tells us we were redeemed "that you may declare the praises of him who called you out of

THE HUGE IDEA:

TRUE WORSHIP BEGINS AT THE CROSS OF CHRIST.

darkness into his wonderful light" (1 Peter 2:9, NIV). God loves turning rebels into worshipers—for what could possibly bring Him more glory than that?

God wants you to know Him intimately and to live a life that's fully alive, awakened to His great love.

>> Who, Not Where

God doesn't require ornate or elaborate expressions of worship. When we talk to Him we don't have to use supersized church words. The worship He's looking for is spiritual and true. Genuine. Authentic. Worship from the heart.

That's how Jesus put it in a conversation He was having with a woman one afternoon while resting beside a common well.

Soon into their talk, Jesus was disclosing His knowledge of her private affairs. (After she mentioned that she was unmarried, He pointed out that she'd actually had five husbands, and the man she was now living with wasn't one of them!) That immediately tipped her off that this guy had some kind of special wisdom. She might as well tap into it.

God wants you to know Him intimately and to live a life that's fully alive, awakened to His great love.

She quickly posed a question that evidently had been bothering her for some time. Her people (the Samaritans) worshiped on one mountain, His people (the Jews) on another. Who was right? Which mountain was better? Where should she worship?

For a total stranger who knew everything about her past, this simple "where" question shouldn't be too hard. Right?

But as we've come to expect, Jesus took the subject to another level, answering her simple "where" question with a riveting "who" answer.

Jesus replied:

> *"Believe me, woman, a time is coming when you will worship the Father neither on this mountain nor in Jerusalem. You Samaritans worship what you do not know* [think UNKNOWN GOD]; *we worship what we do know, for salvation is from the Jews. Yet a time is coming and has now come when the true worshipers will worship the Father in spirit and truth, for they are the kind*

*of worshipers the Father seeks. God is
spirit, and his worshipers must worship in
spirit and in truth.*" (John 4:21–24, NIV)

Wow!

After that, I'm surprised the woman could gather herself to speak, but she did: "I know that Messiah" (called Christ) "is coming. When he comes, he will explain everything to us."

(To which I say, "Lady, you're getting very warm!") But to which Jesus replied, "I who speak to you am he." In other words, Jesus was saying, "I am the Messiah, the sent One from God, sitting right in front of you!" And He's right in front of you and me, too.

Jesus has come. Messiah is here. And He's announcing that worship isn't about where you do it, but about the heart. It's not about what church you belong to, but whether or not you have a personal relationship with God.

The kind of worshipers God is looking for are those who will worship Him as their Father—in spirit and truth.

To worship God *in spirit* requires that we be alive on the inside, experiencing the life He gives by spiritual birth. Without His life, you can never truly worship.

And to worship *in truth* means to worship God as He really is, bringing more than our words—bringing words amplified by an authentic life that flows from being spiritually alive within.

>> Awaken to God's Invitation

But how do you get this inside aliveness? How can we possibly worship in spirit and truth?

Notice how Jesus begins His answer. How He begins God's invitation to a whole new way of worship. Jesus opens with the words, "Believe Me."

For all of us, that's where true worship begins.

This past Sunday at church I was blown away again by the kindness of God. On this particular Sunday it wasn't my pastor's message that got to me, though his message was amazing as always. It wasn't the music. It wasn't even the day's "global theme," though that fueled again my passion for God's glory in all the earth.

What do you think it means to worship in spirit? In truth?

No, on this particular Sunday the story for me was a woman singing in a small vocal choir backing up the worship band. We were all standing and worshiping to David Crowder's version of "Make a Joyful Noise," and the place was rocking. As we sang, the camera focused on a woman in the choir named Lori. She was passionately worshiping God with a huge smile that beautifully reflected the joy we were singing about.

As Lori's face filled the big screen, my eyes filled with tears.

I know Lori from 7|22, a Bible study I taught in Atlanta for ten years. Geared toward young singles, 7|22 draws thousands of them every week to worship from all across our city. Being a middle-aged mom, Lori didn't exactly fit the typical profile of young people. But her teenage son kept inviting her, and she finally came.

Lori was divorced. She was wounded. And she was spiritually lost.

But she came.

Can you see it? A mom with a lot of baggage walking into a room packed with young people with her teen son, wall to wall people going after Jesus.

Something about the place made her feel at home. The spirit she sensed among us drew her in. Pretty soon her eyes were opened to the love and grace of God, and on one spring Tuesday night Lori personally connected with God. Praying a simple prayer, she placed her faith in Christ for eternal life. In an instant she was alive, starting a new journey with God.

Well, that part of the story is amazing enough… but it gets better. It turns out Lori's ex-husband, the teenager's dad, was searching, too. His journey is like so many—a broken childhood and shattered dreams, with deep and desperate wounds leading him down every dead-end road on the planet. In his words, he was "a hard case." A lost cause.

But the transformation happening in Lori's life was too much to ignore, and soon he was opening his heart to the Savior and joining the ranks at 7|22. He, too, became a follower of Christ.

CIRCLE THE WORD BIBLE STUDY

(Circle the word that stands out/means most to you and be ready to talk about why you chose that word.)

I waited patiently for the Lord, he turned to me and heard my cry. He lifted me out of the slimy pit, out of the mud and mire; he set my feet on a rock and gave me a firm place to stand. He put a new song in my mouth, a hymn of praise to our God. Many will see and fear and put their trust in the Lord. PSALM 40:1-3, NIV

God began to restore the relationship between them, and about a year after Lori became a Christian, they were remarried. They started coming to church on Sundays and both were baptized, an expression of the new life they had found in Christ.

A marriage salvaged. Lives restored. A family mended. And two hearts fully alive to worship the God who made them.

Flash back to Sunday morning at my church. Now here's Lori, in the choir, leading the church to worship the Living God!

How could we expect less from God? He's always bringing the dead back to life. Giving the lost unending purpose. Turning rebels into worshipers. Awakening praise from the pits. Putting a song of true worship in our hearts. Allowing us to worship Him as God…and Father.

It's like David said: "I waited patiently for the Lord; he turned to me and heard my cry. He lifted me…out of the mud and mire; he set my feet on a rock.… He put a new song in my mouth, a hymn of praise to our God" (Psalm 40:1–3, NIV).

Watching Lori sing a new song that morning

WIRED Idea: Use a real-life illustration from your own life or the life of your youth ministry to illustrate this point. It may be powerful to actually interview a person on video and show that video to your students.

broke my heart with tears of joy.

That's what the power of the gospel is all about.

>> The Wonderful Cross

But such a transformation in anyone's life comes at a very high price. God doesn't let us worship Him for free. Our worship cost Him the life of His only Son. Bringing us from death to life required someone besides us paying the ultimate penalty for our sin.

That's why at the center of all true worship stands a wonderful cross...the cross on which the Son of God died.[1]

But how can that cross be called wonderful? Isn't it a scene of shame? Isn't its beam a place of suffering?

Absolutely. The Roman cross was a cruel and painful ending. It was a place of execution. Rusted nails. Pierced flesh. Gasping breath.

The cross meant humiliation. Judgment. The cross was agony. A place where people hung until breathing and heartbeats ceased.

Jesus experienced the most horrific death imaginable. There's nothing wonderful about how He died.

What's wonderful about His cross is why He died.

Something truly amazing was happening that day as God offered a ransom for the whole world—Jesus *becoming* sin and shame, suffering and dying for you and me.

To some, it may have appeared that Jesus was being railroaded through the courts of justice and taken by sheer force to die among common criminals. But that's not how it happened.

No one took Jesus' life. He laid it down, willingly satisfying the wrath of a holy God. He chose the cross in order to demonstrate that God was both loving and just. He gave His life so we could receive ours back again. Men may have driven the nails through His hands and feet, but He died because God was sacrificing His only Son.

CIRCLE THE WORD BIBLE STUDY

(Circle the word that stands out/means most to you and be ready to talk about why you chose that word.)

But now [Jesus] has appeared once for all at the end of the ages to do away with sin by the sacrifice of himself. Just as man is destined to die once, and after that face judgment, so Christ was sacrificed once to take away the sins of many people; and he will appear a second time, not to bear sin, but to bring salvation to those who are waiting for him. HEBREWS 9:26B-28, NIV

The cross was the Father's determined end for His Son. The cross was God's idea…God's redemption plan. The cross was the way to open the door. The cross was the only way rebels could ever truly worship again.

Yes, it's a bloodstained cross, but a wonderful cross. In fact, it's the most beautiful thing I've ever seen.

The cross of Christ is a cross of healing. A place of unconditional love. A place of sweet embrace. From His cross comes salvation's song, declaring to all that redemption is here. From it flows forgiveness free. The cross of Christ is a place of peace.

It's the place where true worship begins.

In fact, even as Jesus was dying, worship was very near.

Check it out in Mark's account. A Roman centurion was standing there, doing his job while

The **cross** was the **only** way **rebels** could ever **truly worship** again.

WIRED Idea: How significant is the cross in history? Consider this:

How did Buddha die?
- The Buddha died when he was eighty years old.
- The death was triggered by his physical reaction to a dish of wild mushroom. He died peacefully and mindfully.

How did Muhammad die?
- Muhammad suffered from fever and unknown disease before his death, according to history books.
- He died at sixty-three years of age.

Now think about this: Have you ever seen anyone walking through the halls of your school with a mushroom or thermometer hanging around their neck? Have you ever seen anyone wearing a cross necklace? Why is there such a difference?

Jesus breathed His last breath. As Jesus died, the heavens rumbled and darkened and the earth shook with awe. All of creation shuddered at the sight.

Then, witnessing the greatest act of mercy history has ever known, this Roman soldier—who with his companions had stripped, beaten, mocked, and crucified Jesus—was compelled to proclaim, "Truly this man was the Son of God!" (Mark 15:39).

Amazing! This supposed enemy of Christ was the first of many to have his eyes opened to God's redemption story. He was the first among us to see the wonder of it all.

In a heartbeat, right there in the midst of the stench and sorrow, worship began at the foot of the cross.

At the beginning of WIRED you wrote your own definition of worship. In the space below write your definition of worship WITHOUT looking back at your earlier definition. Once you are finished, compare the two definitions. Do they differ? How?

ADDITIONAL DISCUSSION QUESTIONS

CHAPTER 4: WHAT GOD WANTS MOST FOR YOU

1. How can God think so highly of Himself and not be egotistical or conceited?

2. "God wants you to know Him intimately ," this chapter reminds us, "and to live a life that's fully alive, awakened to His great love." What does this tell you most about God? About you?

3. What helps you most to understand and appreciate how the cross is wonderful? How have you experienced more meaningful worship because of understanding this? How would you describe the place that the cross should have in our worship?

4. As Jesus talked to the Samaritan woman about worship, He began with the words, "Believe Me...." In our lives, how much does true worship depend on our believing God?

5. Think again about all that Jesus told this woman. Which parts of His message to her are most meaningful to you, and why?

6. Bible passages to explore together: John 4:5–26; Mark 15:33–39; Hebrews 10:22.

CHAPTER 5: JOINING THE RANKS OF TRUE WORSHIPERS

In October of 2001, an Albuquerque policeman and his pilot faced disciplinary measures after using a police helicopter to swoop in for a midnight snack of doughnuts. The officer and the civilian pilot were on night patrol over the city in a Kiowa OH-58 helicopter when they landed in a vacant lot next to a Krispy Kreme doughnut store around one o'clock on a Thursday morning.

A spokesman for the Albuquerque Police Department stated that the contracted pilot and a police officer landed the copter early in the morning, ran in and grabbed a dozen, came back out, and took off.

The event was being investigated as a possible misuse of city funds as well as for safety reasons, although it was added there was no specific protocol for this case because it had never happened before.

An eyewitness told the Albuquerque Journal that he saw the APD helicopter circle the Krispy Kreme and land in a nearby dirt field.

"I was angry, and I'm still kind of angry. That's my tax dollars, your tax dollars. You've got no business flying in to get doughnuts," said Keith Turner, who works nearby and was taking a smoke break when he saw the chopper swoop in. The cost to the department of running a Kiowa, including fuel and maintenance, is eighty dollars an hour.

A Krispy Kreme employee who asked not to be identified said he didn't see why people were making a big deal of the unusual doughnut run.

"Cops got to eat, too," he said.[v]

What other youth workers are saying about worship:

—Worship is everything for Him.

—Worship is living all of life—or at least making an honest attempt every day—to bring glory to God!

JOINING THE RANKS OF TRUE WORSHIPERS

THE HUGE IDEA:

WORSHIP STARTS WITH SEEING GOD.

TRUE WORSHIP BEGINS AT
THE CROSS OF CHRIST.

WE NEED TO WORSHIP GOD MORE THAN
GOD NEEDS OUR WORSHIP.

WE ARE MADE TO WORSHIP GOD.

EVERYBODY WORSHIPS SOMETHING.

My hope is that somewhere in the pages

of this book you'll find yourself moving closer and closer to the kind of person Jesus calls a "true worshiper," those who worship the Father from the heart with all they are...all they have.

You may be like the woman Jesus met by the well that day—more concerned with your "place" of worship than the God you meet there.

Or you may be like Lori once was, feeling far away from the love of God.

You might be just waking up to the idea of worship in the first place, only now realizing it's that thing you've been doing your whole life long. Only now sensing you need to redirect its flow.

Or maybe you're a passionate lover of God, but frustrated by the presence of little idols you've kept around far too long.

For all of us, the time for true worship is now. The door is open. The price has been paid. Jesus is here.

THE HUGE IDEA:

WORSHIP STARTS

WITH SEEING GOD.

>> Making the Move

So while the whole world is busy glorifying who knows what, God is inviting any and all to join the ranks of the true worshipers—those who are beginning to discover the connection between His infinite worth and their own inner longing to love something supremely.

We began this book by seeing that worship is our response to what we value most. That's the basic, entry-level definition, describing the kind of worship everybody does all the time. That definition is like Webster's, as he defines worship as "extreme devotion or intense love or admiration of any kind."

But now we're going deeper. Now we're making the move from worshiping any god that dangles in our view to responding to the invitation of the matchless God of gods. Now we're talking about a brand of worship that's lasting and true. The kind we were made for. Worship that both honors God and satisfies us.

For this we need a bigger definition, one that will take us deeper as we move together toward a life of true worship.

Here we go—

Worship is…
our response,
both personal and corporate,
to God—
for who He is!
and what He has done!
expressed in and by the things we say
and the way we live.

Granted, it's not real catchy and concise. But then again, we're not taking on a tiny subject. The definition may be a mouthful, but I like it. And as we dig down to uncover its meaning, it will give us a lot to think about together.

In a nutshell, it's saying worship is a whole-life response to God's greatness and glory.

>> It's Something You Do

Worship is a verb. Or so says worship author Robert Webber.

I think he's right. Practically speaking, *worship*

Worship is a
whole-life response
to **God's greatness**
and **glory**.

is always a verb. Worship is something you do.

Worship isn't something you *watch*, contrary to the thinking of many of us who attend church. That may be hard to believe, given that in most churches the rows of seats (or pews) are arranged so that you have the best view of what's happening onstage. If that's not enough, the action is often magnified on the big screens. The lights also point to the platform. And to help you with your viewing pleasure, you're handed a program at the door—a lineup card for what's happening in today's "show," if you will. After all, it's all put on for your enjoyment, right?

But here's a news flash for you. Worship isn't something you attend, like a movie or a concert. Worship is something you enter into with all your might. Worship is a participation sport in a spectator culture.

Check out the Psalms, both the longest book in the entire Bible and the one that deals almost exclusively with the subject of worship. The Psalms are filled with verbs:

Shout to God. Sing a new song. Dance before

WIRED Idea: Take some time and watch religious programming, whether a church service or a Christian channel on television. How is what you observe different from the WIRED definition of worship? Is it different at all? Why or why not? What did you think and feel while watching?

What are some ways God has been making Himself known to you recently. Do you sense Him pursuing you? Why or why not?

Him. Clap your hands. Bow down. Lift up your heads. Tell of His might. Stand in awe. Meditate on His truth. Walk in His ways. Still your heart. Cast down your idols. Run to Him. Make a loud noise. Lift your hands. Strike up the band (okay, so that one's a bit modernized). Clash the cymbals. Praise Him with trumpet sound. Seek His face. Tell the nations.

True worship is a whole-life response to God's greatness and glory. A response that taps our mind, our soul, our heart of passion…and all our strength.

>> It Doesn't Start with Us

I think the key word in our new definition is *response*.

Worship is our response to God. In other words, we don't initiate worship; God does.

> He reveals; we respond.
> He discloses; we respond.
> He unveils; we respond.
> He chooses to show us how amazing
>   He is; we say, "God, You're amazing!"

Our whole relationship with God works the same way:

He loves. We love in return.
He calls. We answer.
He leads. We follow.

>> If Only You Were There

Several years ago Shelley and I were at a youth camp in Texas, hanging out one afternoon by the senior high pool. (Yes, they had their own pool—middle schoolers once again get the raw end of the deal!) About fifty students stood in the shallow end while four or five of their friends were putting on a diving exhibition at the other.

This camp's pool still had a high dive (not too common in our lawsuit-driven culture). And the brave few were taking their turns entertaining the rest. I remember two of them as if I were sitting there now.

One guy was "*so together*." Must have been a gymnast—he was ripped and fit, with perfect "pool hair" and even better form. A typical dive for him would begin with the "Olympic pause" on the very last fraction of the board, then continue with various twists and tucks and turns. Like a missile he would knife into the water, then quickly swim to the side and lean back and shake his wonderful hair as he nonchalantly strutted back to the diving board's ladder.

He was cocky. But he was good.

But another guy was stealing the show. He couldn't dive like "pretty boy" if he had to, but that hardly mattered.

He was robust, full of life, a tad heavy, and sporting yellow surf shorts that hung well below his knees. After each of Mr. Perfect's successive attempts, this guy would appear. Not too bright, but fearless nonetheless, he would fly off the board like mad.

Can you see him? On this particular turn, the guy in the yellow shorts is doing a "watermelon" from fifteen feet up, proceeding to splash everyone in the shallow end of the pool.

Everybody's laughing. Everyone's smiling. He's

making the afternoon a lot of fun at the senior high pool.

But on his next attempt, things turn ugly. Fast.

This time he's flying off into the air with a little extra boost, but it quickly becomes apparent to all that he hasn't exactly thought through this maneuver before leaving the diving board.

Soon he's in midflight, parallel with the water, no more revolutions to take place, and on the way down. Faceup and stretched out, he has lost the battle with gravity—and the pool is getting closer by the second.

At this point I turned my attention to the audience of students in the shallow end of the pool. By the expressions on their faces, I could tell something awful was about to happen. Their eyes were getting wider and wider. An eerie quiet settled over the entire pool.

Then I heard it: *SPLAT!* You've heard it before—the horrible sound of human flesh solidly smacking the water.

At once—as if somehow the minds of everyone watching had been melded into one—a groan emerged from deep inside each person: *UUHHHhhhhhhh!*

It was one of the most together things I've ever seen.

It was if they were being led, almost like someone had been doing a play-by-play commentary, then orchestrating their response: "Okay, everyone, he's coming down! He's at ten feet and dropping like lead—eight feet, I'm thinking ugly—four, get ready to groan—three, he's gonna hit hard—two, it's going to be a back-buster—one—let's hear it all together…NOW!"

UUHHHhhhhhhh!

But there was no director there that day telling the students what to do and when to do it. What they did was natural, the most appropriate response to what they were seeing. It was spontaneous. Their response was true.

And no matter how vividly I try to describe what happened on that summer afternoon, I couldn't possibly get you to respond with the same agony and intensity that they did. Sure, you may cringe a little just hearing about it; but to respond as they did in that moment, you had to have seen what they were seeing.

Talk about a time in your life when you REALLY saw God clearly. How did this affect your worship?

WIRED Idea: Find a picture or video clip that should and will elicit a response from students. Maybe it is a funny video. Maybe it is a picture of a gruesome injury or strange but true event. Show it to your students and watch how they respond. Then connect their response to the idea of worship being our response to who God is and what He has done.

>> Look Up

The same thing that was true in the pool that after-noon is true of our worship today. Unless we see God, we cannot worship Him. Worship is what spontaneously flows out of us when we come face-to-face with Him. It's the natural response to all of who He is—our uncalculated response to all He has done.

Sure, we get a massive amount out of the experience of worshiping Him. But at its core, worship is all about God. It's *for* Him. Our worship is *to* Him.

That's why we say—

> Worship is…
> *our response,*
> both personal and corporate,
> *to God—*
> for who He is!
> and what He has done!

Circle the word or words in this definition that jump out at you most.

So often in the Psalms we find expressions very similar to this one: "Great is the Lord and greatly to be praised." When you break it all down, true worship is simply catching sight of the greatness, majesty, glory, and grace of an infinite God.

When God is not greatly praised, it's only because we don't think He's that great of a God. When our worship is small, it's because our concept of God is small. When we offer God little-bitty sacrifices, it's because we've somehow reduced Him in our hearts to a little-bitty God. Our vision has become clouded, our hearts distracted.

As a result, our lives shrivel into insignificance and meaninglessness. We just bump along in this mass of humanity, having no real clue what life's all about. We fret. We get depressed. We worry and get bent out of shape. We go down all kinds of dead-end paths as we try to accomplish everything by ourselves. Sometimes leading to irreversible destruction.

We lose sight of the reality of all realities: There's an infinite, limitless God high and exalted on His throne, ruling with all power and authority

So far, as you've been on the WIRED journey, what have you learned or rediscovered about true worship that's already making a difference in your life?

over the heavens and the earth. A God who's still running the show—running our lives and running the whole universe on His timetable.

And at this very moment, while He holds entire galaxies in place by His power, He also invites us at any time day or night to look up and behold Him as He is. He invites us to call Him by name and be His friend.

ADDITIONAL DISCUSSION QUESTIONS

CHAPTER 5: JOINING THE RANKS OF TRUE WORSHIPERS

1. This chapter tells us that God is the one who initiates worship, not us. What practical difference do you think this makes?

2. Scriptures to explore together: Psalms 95 and 150.

CHAPTER 6: FOR WHO HE IS, FOR WHAT HE DOES

One day a group of scientists got together and decided that man had come a long way and no longer needed God. So they picked one scientist to go and tell Him that they were done with Him.

The scientist walked up to God and said, "God, we've decided that we no longer need you. We're to the point that we can clone people and do many miraculous things, so why don't you just go on and get lost!"

God listened very patiently and kindly to man. After the scientist was done talking, God said, "Very well. How about this? Let's have a man-making contest."

The scientist replied, "Okay. Great!"

But God added, "Now we are going to do this just like I did back in the old days with Adam."

The scientist said, "Sure, no problem!" and bent down and grabbed himself a handful of dirt.

God looked at him and said, "No. No. No. *You go and get your own dirt.*"

What other youth workers are saying about **worship**:

—*Worship is whatever you're living for...whether you know it or not. It is offering your very being and everything you have in radical trust.*

—*Worship is living my life in such a way that others can see that there is something in my life greater than me.*

FOR WHO HE IS, FOR WHAT HE DOES

THE HUGE IDEA:

**WE WORSHIP GOD FOR WHO
HE IS AND WHAT HE HAS DONE.**

WORSHIP STARTS WITH SEEING GOD.

TRUE WORSHIP BEGINS AT
THE CROSS OF CHRIST.

WE NEED TO WORSHIP GOD MORE THAN
GOD NEEDS OUR WORSHIP.

WE ARE MADE TO WORSHIP GOD.

EVERYBODY WORSHIPS SOMETHING.

How can we get a better and higher view

of God in our lives? How can we become the true worshipers we were designed to be? How can we bring back into focus a sense of how awesome God is?

The answer is, we can't. Not on our own, that is. Unless God Himself shows us who He is, we can't respond to Him with true worship from our hearts.

God reveals…so we can respond…in authentic, natural worship.

So what is He showing us? If authentic worship is the natural response to what God has revealed… then what exactly has He revealed about Himself?

Well, this book, and ten thousand like it, could never contain the sum of His greatness and worth. There's no way we could grasp it all. Our minds are too small. The brainpower is not there.

But there's so much we *can* know. Enough, in fact, to keep us exalting Him for a lifetime.

For now, let's just think about two aspects of His character that reveal His heart to you and me.

WIRED Idea: A great passage underscoring the concept of recovering an exalted view of God is Romans 12:1. Read this verse with your students. Now discuss the idea of "in view of God's mercy." What comes to mind when you read those words? How do you keep that in mind?

An illustration option is a clip from the movie *Braveheart* when William Wallace is being put to death. He is asked by the executioner to profess his allegiance to the King of England. And what happens? Wallace sees his beautiful bride in his mind's eye and screams "freedom," sealing his doom.

CIRCLE THE WORD BIBLE STUDY

(Circle the word that stands out/means most to you and be ready to talk about why you chose that word.)

Praise the Lord. Praise God in his sanctuary; praise him in his mighty heavens.

Praise him for his acts of power; praise him for his surpassing greatness. . . .

Let everything that has breath praise the Lord. PSALM 150: 1-2, 6, NIV

>> Infinitely Awesome

We know God is infinitely awesome.

This God with whom we deal is no small fry. He's not our size. Not even somewhat larger. He's not made of the stuff we're made of. He doesn't have to deal with our barriers and limitations.

"Before the mountains were born or You gave birth to the earth and the world, even from everlasting to everlasting, You are God." Notice that the psalmist didn't write, "from everlasting to everlasting You *were* God." But, You *are* God (Psalm 90:2).

What does it mean that God is infinite? Simply…that He *is*. Beyond that, our little brains are hard-pressed for more. We don't really even know what "infinite" is all about. Try to define it.

THE HUGE IDEA:

WE WORSHIP GOD FOR WHO

HE IS AND WHAT HE HAS DONE.

Infinite means having no limits. Never running out.
Having no end. Existing forever. Unbound.
Timeless. Stuff we can't fully comprehend.

God has never been tired. Never slept. Never
aged. Never upgraded.

He's self-sufficient. Self-contained. God doesn't
need anything. Or anybody.

If all of us happen to fall off the face of the
earth, God will still be exactly who He is. If all of
us abandon our worship of Him, He'll remain the
same. God's greatness doesn't depend on us. If not
one single person on earth ever chose to respond to
Him in love, believing in Him and worshiping
Him, God would still be all that He already is,
always has been, and always will be.

*Oh, the depth of the riches both of the
wisdom and knowledge of God! How
unsearchable are His judgments and
unfathomable His ways! For who has
known the mind of the Lord, or who
became His counselor? Or who has first
given to Him that it might be paid*

> God has
> **never** been **tired**.
> Never **aged**.
> Never **upgraded**.

*back to him again? For from Him and
through Him and to Him are all
things. To Him be the glory forever.
Amen.* (Romans 11:33–36)

Science is gaining ground every day. We can
look farther into space and deeper within our bodies
than ever before. And what we discover stuns and
amazes us. We're finding there's more out in space
than we could ever imagine. And more complexity
within our bodies than we can understand.

We've put men on the moon, but we can't quite
make it to Mars, our closest planet neighbor. We
inhabit a galaxy comprised of billions of stars, of
which our mighty sun is average at best. And our
Milky Way is only one galaxy among billions more,
each housing billions of other stars.

We'll never see more than the tiniest fraction of
them. Yet God has given each one a name.

*Lift your eyes and look to the heavens:
Who created all these? He who brings
out the starry host one by one, and calls*

them each by name. Because of his great
power and mighty strength, not one of
them is missing. (Isaiah 40:26, NIV)

And while we wrestle with the cause of it all,
He offers this simple yet irrefutable explanation: "In
the beginning, God created the heavens and the
earth." And why not? If you're as awesome as He is,
why not make a universe that's vast enough to constantly echo Your greatness back to You?

But, more than just making the universe for His
glory, God did it to show Himself to you and me.
"For since the creation of the world God's invisible
qualities—his eternal power and divine nature—
have been clearly seen, being understood from what
has been made, so that men are without excuse"
(Romans 1:20, NIV).

CIRCLE THE WORD BIBLE STUDY

(Circle the word that stands out/means most to you and be ready to talk about why you chose that word.)

Oh, the depth of the riches of the wisdom and knowledge of God! How
unsearchable His judgments, and unfathomable are His ways! Who has known
the mind of the Lord? Or who has been His counselor? Who has ever given to
God, that God should repay Him? For from Him and through Him and to Him
are all things. To Him be glory forever. Amen. ROMANS 11:33-36

Using the word *awesome,* as an adjective, has become common in the conversations of our day. But nothing is really awesome but God alone.

God is awesome in glory. And awesome in holiness. On more than one occasion we glimpse into heaven and hear the angels repeating, "Holy, holy, holy is the Lord Almighty." In fact, holiness is the only one of His attributes that we see angels repeating over and over again. Is it possible that holiness is at the heart of God's God-ness? The center of all of who He is?

God is pure. Radiant. Without blemish or stain. He is untainted goodness. Without fault or blame. Perfection personified.

When You're God, You're always who You are—unchanging, unaffected by anything or anyone. He doesn't change with the crowd, go with the flow, or alter to please somebody else.

>> Intimately Approachable

And if God's infinite nature isn't mind-boggling enough, consider this: The infinitely awesome God is inviting you to draw near Him.

"Who is like the LORD our God, who is enthroned on high, who humbles Himself to behold the things that are in heaven and in the earth?" (Psalm 113:5–6).

Yes, He's enthroned on high, but God has lowered Himself to take notice of our lives. To become, as David said, "intimately acquainted" with all our ways.

Think about it. This great and majestic God is totally aware of every single detail of your life. He's God in heaven, yet He knows everything there is to know about you, things you don't even know about yourself.

What a miraculous thing that we're invited to respond to this incredible God. That the Almighty One has somehow chosen of His own free will to desire your worship. Though He had no real need or obligation to do so, He invites you to draw near to Him and discover who He is.

How can it be that God is infinite in being and power, yet you and I can touch Him? We can touch His heart. We can cause joy to come to Him. Cause Him to smile. We can bring God pleasure. Make Him happy.

Talk about the three or four things that you love and enjoy most about God.

Your worship matters to God.

It's true that "the heavens are telling of the glory of God." But right where you are in this moment, God is there and He's saying, "I want you to tell of My glory, too."

The rocks He has made are capable of singing songs, should He ask them to; but He draws near your side and whispers, "I'd rather hear *you* sing a new song of praise to Me!"

God is constantly surrounded by heavenly throngs and endless praise, yet He says to you and me, "I know your voice, even the thoughts of your heart. And your worship—your arrows of affection—reach My heart."

>> True Worship Always Hangs in the Balance

Infinitely Awesome—Intimately Approachable.

Creator—Father.

Lord Almighty—Friend.

A contradiction? No. A paradox? For sure.

That God is Father and Friend at once is part of His divine mystery—something we're better off not trying to figure out. Instead, we need only embrace the mystery, holding on to what my friend refers to so often as "the friendship and the fear."

If we're going to worship God for who He is, we have to continually live in the tension of these two aspects of His character. If we swing too far to the "approachable" end of the spectrum, we'll eventually reduce God to someone our own size, like the T-shirt that proudly proclaims, "Jesus is my homeboy."

By doing so, we'll dishonor Him and forget who we are. Soon we'll be frustrated by this little god we've made for ourselves. Our worship will shrink like socks in a dryer. And our faith will diminish, robbing us of hope and robbing God of His glory.

But we cannot forgo His invitation to intimacy, either. How can we forget that through the wonder of grace we belong to Him as sons and daughters? We are the loved children of God. We get no extra credit in heaven for keeping Him at arm's length. Especially given the fact He has bulldozed His way through the wall of sin and shame that kept us from Him.

Talk about how you relate to God most often…is it as "homeboy" or Holy God? How can you keep the balance between friendship with God and reverence for Him?

We are His, filled with His Spirit. And His Spirit cries out from within our hearts, "Abba, Father." So we consider how awesome He is, standing in awe of all He has done—and at the same time we boldly embrace Him through the life of His Son, loving Him tenderly like a child in his daddy's hug.

>> And if That's Not Reason Enough

Our worship begins with our response to who God is. But that's not all we have to be thankful for. That's not all we have to celebrate.

Don't get me wrong. If all you ever know about God is what you know right now, you would still know enough to praise Him forever.

But there's more.

In addition to God's infinite character, we praise Him for everything He's done.

CIRCLE THE WORD BIBLE STUDY

(Circle the word that stands out/means most to you and be ready to talk about why you chose that word.)

For you did not receive a spirit that makes you a slave again to fear, but you received the Spirit of sonship. And by him we cry, "Abba, Father." The Spirit himself testifies with our spirit that we are God's children. ROMANS 8:15-16, NIV

Worship is…

> our response,
> both personal and corporate,
> to God—
> for who He is!
> and *what He has done*!

It's the potent combination of these two kinds of praise—praising Him for who He is and what He has done—that cause worship to always be an option for us, no matter what.

When we can't tell what God is up to, and we can't see Him working around in our circumstances, we can still praise Him simply for who we know Him to be. Even if our circumstances don't reveal it, God is still all of who He is. No matter what life sends our way, we focus our attention on Him. He's still God in the midst of joy and tragedy.

In that same way, we can always praise Him for what He has done, though at times we feel we can't quite sense that He is near.

Our lives are filled with gifts from God, little

Does it still make sense to praise God in the midst of hard times and trials? If so, why?

miracles. Flowers *every* spring. The trees that line the road we take to school. The car (new or not so new) that gets us there. A chance to laugh. Eyes to see. A place to sleep. His faithfulness in days gone by. All of these should keep us worshiping moment by moment. Let's face it, gratitude for the gift of breath alone should keep us praising for quite some time!

We praise God for who He is.

We honor Him for all He has done.

Even if God never does another thing for us, should we cease to worship? Of course not—not when we remember all that He's already done through the gift of His Son.

No matter what life sends our way, we **focus** our attention on **Him**. He's **still** a **good** and **gracious God** in the midst of **joy and tragedy**.

ADDITIONAL DISCUSSION QUESTIONS

CHAPTER 6: FOR WHO HE IS, FOR WHAT HE DOES

1. What are your best answers for the three questions that this chapter begins with: "How can we get a better and higher view of God in our lives? How can we become the true worshipers we were designed to be? How can we bring back into focus a sense of how awesome God is?"

2. When have you been most captivated by and excited about God's character—about who He is?

3. When have you been most captivated by and excited about God's actions—about what He has done or is doing?

4. What have you found to be the most important factors in protecting and nurturing the intimacy of your relationship with God?

5. Passages from God's Word to explore: Psalm 90:1–2; Romans 11:33–36; Psalm 113; Romans 8:15.

CHAPTER 7: WORSHIP AS A WAY OF LIFE

On the afternoon of April 18, 1775, a young boy who worked at a stable in Boston overheard two British army officers talking. When he heard something about there being "hell to pay tomorrow," he ran with the news to Boston's North End to the home of a silversmith named Paul Revere. What happened in the hours and days after this seemingly insignificant encounter serves as an anchor for our history as Americans. We have learned since childhood in school of the famous midnight ride of Paul Revere. But have you ever heard of William Dawes?

I didn't think so…

You see, there were actually two men that rode that fateful night to warn the towns and colonial leaders north and west of Boston. Paul Revere we know. In every town he passed through, church bells rang, drums started beating, and the news of the British's intent on Lexington and Concord spread like a virus, so much so that a ragtag band of militia confronted and soundly defeated the British the next day. But William Dawes?

He rode west of Boston at the same time Revere began his ride north. He was carrying the same urgent message through just as many towns and just as many miles. Yet only one made a lasting and effective impression—and Dawes was not that man. He fluttered into anonymity like an oak leaf on a blustery fall day. But why?[vi]

History tells us that Paul Revere had been passionate about the cause of freedom long before that night. His ride was an extension of a life consumed with freedom. And people listened and responded. Our worship risks Dawes's fate unless we understand that the cross demands worship that is whole life and not simply Sunday morning.

What other youth workers are saying about worship:

—*Worship is honoring God through obedience in every facet of my life.*

—*Worship is choosing to live my life for God, giving my best to Him in whatever I do—giving Him all the thanks and applause.*

WORSHIP AS A WAY OF LIFE

THE HUGE IDEA:

ALL WORSHIP INVOLVES SACRIFICE.

WE WORSHIP GOD FOR WHO
HE IS AND WHAT HE HAS DONE.

WORSHIP STARTS WITH SEEING GOD.

TRUE WORSHIP BEGINS AT
THE CROSS OF CHRIST.

WE NEED TO WORSHIP GOD MORE THAN
GOD NEEDS OUR WORSHIP.

WE ARE MADE TO WORSHIP GOD.

EVERYBODY WORSHIPS SOMETHING.

Which would you prefer?

A dad who tells you how important you are *OR* a dad who actually shows up for the important stuff in your life?

Friends who keep reminding you how tight you are *OR* friends who are there when you need them most, never stabbing you in the back?

A "significant other" who makes you really cool homemade cards telling you you're the best thing that has ever happened to them *OR* one who respects you, keeps your trust, and doesn't date around on you?

Someone who tells you how special you are *OR* someone who shows you?

Well, if you're like me, the answer is…BOTH! I want the words *and* the actions, and I'm guessing the same can be said about you.

Well, God is no different than you and me. The worship God is after is a BOTH kind of worship. He wants our words *and* our actions.

We see this in the two primary words that are used for worship in the New Testament.

THE HUGE IDEA:

ALL WORSHIP

INVOLVES SACRIFICE.

Jesus used one of them in His conversation with the Samaritan woman beside the well. This word we translate "worship" is all about an attitude of honor and reverence. It means literally "to bow before," or "to kiss the hand of a king."

The other worship-word has a much less glamorous meaning. It simply means to serve.

It's the word Paul uses in Romans 12:1–2, a central NT passage on worship. He begins by begging us "In view of God's mercy, to offer our bodies as living sacrifices, holy and pleasing to God." This, Paul declares, is our "spiritual act of worship." Or literally, our spiritual act of "service."

Paul was saying, If you've seen mercy…if you've seen the cross…then offer all of who you are to God in response to all that He has done.

Let's face it: That kind of full-blown serving is not usually the first thing we think of when we think of worship. But in God's economy worship = serving. Worship = life.

But in
God's economy
worship = **serving**.
Worship = **life**.

CIRCLE THE WORD BIBLE STUDY

(Circle the word that stands out/means most to you and be ready to talk about why you chose that word.)

Therefore I urge you, brothers, in view of God's mercy, to offer your bodies as living sacrifices, holy and pleasing to God—this is your spiritual act of worship.

ROMANS 12:1, NIV

>> What We Can Do

What God has revealed to us about Himself is beyond our words of gratitude. What He has done on our behalf makes it impossible for us to ever repay Him.

But what we *can* do in return—and must do—is give Him everything we have through a life of service to Him and to those around us.

That's what we mean when we say worship is a way of life.

For far too long, people have been cheating God, somehow thinking that if they just keep telling Him He's great, He'll be content. Whether their words are genuine doesn't seem to matter. Whether their lives back up their words is no big deal.

After all, words come so easy. And saying (and singing) them makes us feel a little better about ourselves, even when our hearts don't back up the words coming from our lips.

But God isn't honored by words alone. Like any of us, He's moved by words that are authenticated by actions. When it comes to worship, it's the total package that matters—what you say, how you say it, and whether you mean it. And our words mean most when they're amplified by the way we choose to live our lives when we are faced with various opportunities and temptations.

Worship is…

> our response,
> both personal and corporate,
> to God—
> for who He is!
> and what He has done!
> expressed in and by *the things we say*
>   *and the way we live.*

On Sunday morning you may be singing with all you've got, maybe even falling on your knees to tell God He's your "all in all." But the whole time God may be thinking, "There seem to be a lot of other things in your life lately that you desire a whole lot more than Me."

In that moment, we are no different from those of ages past about whom God said, "These people honor me with their lips, but their hearts are far from me" (Isaiah 29:13, NIV).

God is no dummy. He knows what's going on in our hearts. And God knows how easy it is for us to say one thing and do another. That's why the true test of worship isn't so much what we say, but how we live.

If it's true that God sees and knows our hearts, why are we afraid to be honest in our worship?

>> How Can We Offer Less?

God has given us "life and breath and all things," as Paul told those guys in Athens. The only fitting response to all He has done is to give back to Him all that we are. Anything less is not enough. Anything less is not true worship. Anything less only proves that we haven't really seen Him at all.

Take, for instance, His mercy and grace.

We deserved death, but received life. God's grace and mercy are really just that simple.

So how do we respond to the cross of Christ?

With a Sunday visit to church?

By dropping two bucks in the offering plate?

Singing a few verses of a chorus we love?

By lifting our hands?

Dropping in on the Christian club at school?

Wearing a cross?

Why do you think we offer God such small sacrifices of worship?

Owning a Bible?

Showing up for youth group a few times a month?

No way! The only right response to such mercy and grace is our *everything*. All our time, all our decisions, everything we say and are.

>> I'm the Offering

Somewhere in the modern culture we've become confused, thinking that *worship* and *songs* are one and the same. In other words we think singing songs = worship and worship = singing songs.

The church scene is flooded with new worship songs. That's not a bad thing in and of itself. But it's deadly when we make a subtle mental shift and

WIRED Idea: God has given us "life and breath and all things." The only fitting response to all He has done is to give back to Him all that we are. Anything less is not enough. Anything less is not true worship. Anything less only proves that we haven't really seen Him at all.

Part of the reason we do not respond to God with everything is because we do not see ourselves in need. When you live in such an affluent culture, the need to abandon yourself to God seems silly and hyper. Yet anything less than all is not true worship.

Here is a great way to illustrate this tension: Have two gift-wrapped boxes or two gift bags. Students should not be able to tell what the gifts are. Make the two gifts something similar to the following: a banana as one gift and a Walkman or iPod (something expensive and of worth) as the other.

Give the student the banana in a gift bag first and ask them to open it. Once they open it, ask if they want to exchange for another gift or keep the banana. If they choose to keep the banana, show them what they could have had. If they choose to exchange, they have exchanged for something greater.

Here is the point: Without Christ, we are bananas. When we understand that we are nothing without Christ, that He has given us life and breath and all things, and we exchange our nature for Christ, we become rich in God. And when you understand your wealth in Christ—what you get in the exchange—you respond accordingly.

Most students live as if the gift of God is like a bundle of bananas.

start believing that by singing the songs, we're worshiping in truth.

Don't get me wrong. I'm all for worship songs—both old and new.

Singing songs about the cross is fine. It's actually a very good thing. A biblical thing. Something much needed in the church.

But a song alone is not enough.

The cross demands more.

Grace requires that we bring ourselves, laying our lives before this merciful God.

This wholehearted, full-on, life-encompassing response to God's amazing grace is the "reasonable" thing to do.

Giving God everything is our only reasonable response.

Now, check out Paul's challenging words again, this time from a contemporary paraphrase:

> So here's what I want you to do, God
> helping you: Take your everyday, ordinary life—your sleeping, eating,
> going-to-work, and walking-around

life—and place it before God as an offering. Embracing what God does for you is the best thing you can do for him. (Romans 12:1, *The Message*)

That's it! Worshiping God is what we do as we respond to His mercy in our "walking-around life."

> *It's not the words I sing,*
> *but me I bring;*
> *I'm the offering laid at Your feet,*
> *My steps the melody, oh so sweet,*
> *All of me in praise of Thee.*[2]

Worship is life!

Grace requires that we bring ourselves, **laying our lives** before this **merciful God**.

ADDITIONAL DISCUSSION QUESTIONS

CHAPTER 7: WORSHIP AS A WAY OF LIFE

1. Think about the word "service." What kind of thoughts and impressions—either positive or negative—does it bring to mind?

2. What motivates you most to want to offer yourself fully to God?

3. This chapter includes this statement: "Grace requires that we bring ourselves, laying our lives before this merciful God." Is grace really grace if it has this or any requirement attached to it? What do you think?

4. How can we know that we're genuinely honoring God and pleasing Him? How can we be sure?

5. Bible passages to explore and experience together: Romans 6:13; 12:1–2.

CHAPTER 8: THROUGH JESUS, ALL THE TIME

You are the parent of an eight-year-old girl named Molly. Her two best friends, Amy and Imani, both live nearby. As Molly's parent, you know that Amy's parents keep a gun in their house, so you have forbidden Molly to play there. Instead, Molly spends a lot of time at Imani's house, which has a swimming pool in the backyard. You feel good about having made such a smart choice to protect your daughter. After all, your task as her parent is to make sure that she plays and stays in safe environments.

According to the data, however, your choice isn't smart at all. In a given year, there is one drowning of a child for every 11,000 residential pools in the United States. In a country of 6 million pools, this means that roughly 550 children under the age of ten drown each year.

Meanwhile, there is 1 child killed by a gun for every 1 million-plus guns. In a country with an estimated 200 million guns, this means that roughly 175 children under ten die each year from guns. The likelihood of death by pool (1 in 11,000) versus death by gun (1 in 1 million-plus) isn't even close: Molly is roughly 100 times more likely to die in a swimming accident at Imani's house than in gunplay at Amy's.[vii]

Facts unknown to you make your choice a bad one. What you cannot see and do not know may take your child's life. These may only be statistics, but a similar unseen force is working within you. But if you do not recognize it for what it is—the undeniable reality that you and I were uniquely made to be exceptional worshipers of God—then your choice of what to make your focus will be misguided. And, like that 8-year-old girl, you may be exposing yourself to danger just when you think you are safe.

Makes you think, doesn't it?

What other youth workers are saying about **worship**:

—*Worship is the life we live as we are completely astonished by the glory of God.*

—*Worship is my life lived to the fullest for God as a living sacrifice.*

THROUGH JESUS, ALL THE TIME

THE HUGE IDEA:

**JESUS MAKES OUR WORSHIP
ACCEPTABLE TO GOD.**

ALL WORSHIP INVOLVES SACRIFICE.

WE WORSHIP GOD FOR WHO
HE IS AND WHAT HE HAS DONE.

WORSHIP STARTS WITH SEEING GOD.

TRUE WORSHIP BEGINS AT
THE CROSS OF CHRIST.

WE NEED TO WORSHIP GOD MORE THAN
GOD NEEDS OUR WORSHIP.

WE ARE MADE TO WORSHIP GOD.

EVERYBODY WORSHIPS SOMETHING.

As I have continued to try and grasp

the fullness of what worship is all about over the years, this passage of Scripture has consistently captured my attention:

> *Through Him then, let us continually offer up a sacrifice of praise to God, that is, the fruit of lips that give thanks to His name. And do not neglect doing good and sharing, for with such sacrifices God is pleased.* (Hebrews 13:15–16)

We know by the context of the surrounding verses that the "Him" in the first phrase refers to Jesus.

I think the meaning hits us more forcefully when His name is included in the text:

Through Jesus then, let us continually offer up a sacrifice of praise to God, that is the fruit of lips that give thanks to His name. And do not neglect doing good and sharing, for with such sacrifices God is pleased.

THE HUGE IDEA:

JESUS MAKES OUR WORSHIP

ACCEPTABLE TO GOD.

It all happens because of (through) Jesus.

Jesus is the everlasting door by which we come to worship God.

>> No More Religious Systems

We're no longer under any religious system. Not that of the Old Testament system of law and sacrifice, or any other. In the past, God-worshipers had to approach Him through a very specific religious system of "do's" and "don'ts." But not anymore.

Christ is the final offering for sin; He offered "one sacrifice for sins for all time" (Hebrews 10:12). So as we come to worship the Father, we aren't required to bring a sacrifice in an attempt to make us right with God. Jesus has already done that for us.

This truth is important to grasp because we consistently fail to live as we should live. And when we fail, the enemy is quick to condemn us, telling us we can't possibly be a worshiper after what we've done.

CIRCLE THE WORD BIBLE STUDY

(Circle the word that stands out/means most to you and be ready to talk about why you chose that word.)

Through Him then, let us continually offer a sacrifice of praise to God, that is, the fruit of lips that give thanks to His name. And do not neglect doing good and sharing with others, for with such sacrifices God is pleased. HEBREWS 13:15-16, NIV

But those words are lies. We can always come back to God in worship, no matter where we've been or how far we've fallen.

How can that be?

Because we come through Jesus Christ. His death makes it possible for us to be accepted by God. His cross makes our worship acceptable in the Father's sight. Through Jesus Christ we can approach His throne of grace. Anytime. Anywhere.

That's why a huge awareness of the cross is almost always in my mind as I come to worship. And when it's not, the Holy Spirit puts it there. Fast.

>> Nail Open the Door

How can I embrace this awesome God of wonder and not cherish the cross that allows me to approach Him in the first place?

So many people don't know the fullness of what Christ has done for them. The greatness of who He has made them to be. They don't know enough about their new standing with God in Christ in order to break free from the lies of the deceiver.

They try to worship, but condemnation chokes

WIRED Idea: With parental consent, watch *The Passion of the Christ* with your students. Ask them the following questions:

- What did the crucifixion scenes mean to you?
- How do those six hours affect your life today?

out their praise. Guilt restrains their hearts. Shame stifles their songs.

No wonder their worship is weak and lame. No wonder so many aren't shouting His praise or breaking out in a dance of unrestrained celebration.

Maybe we're not getting the gospel—the whole gospel. We're shortsighted.

In Jesus Christ we're free! We are eternally forgiven. Rescued. Washed clean. Made new. Re-created.

There's no more condemnation for anyone in Christ Jesus. He's our life. His righteousness is our righteousness. We're born again. Children of God. Permanently attached to Him. Our debt is paid in full. Sin's power is broken. Death is defeated. We're alive!

These are the truths that nail open the doorway into God's presence. And, you, too, can come through that door to worship. Not because of your goodness or righteousness. But because of the cross of Christ.

CIRCLE THE WORD BIBLE STUDY

(Circle the word that stands out/means most to you and be ready to talk about why you chose that word.)

Therefore, there is now no condemnation for those who are in Christ Jesus, because through Christ Jesus the law of the Spirit of life set me free from the law of sin and death. ROMANS 8:1-2, NIV

>> You Can't Be Serious

We always come to worship through the doorway of Jesus Christ. But check out what comes next in that Hebrews 13 passage: "Through Jesus then, let us continually offer up a sacrifice of praise to God."

Hello! Are you seeing what I'm seeing?

This verse says we are to worship *continually*!

God's got to be kidding, right?

Continually offer Him a sacrifice of praise? Like 24/7? Day and night? All the time? How is that even possible?

Maybe we should all join a monastery. Or maybe not. Maybe we should just take a deep breath and consider what the writer of these verses is suggesting.

For one, he's making a massive point with his first-century readers who were quite familiar with the smells and sights of animal sacrifices. They knew what it meant to come once a week, or once a year, bringing some animal as an offering to God.

But it's not like that anymore. We're not talking about a once-a-week or twice-a-year thing. We're talking about a new relationship that allows us to praise God at any moment, in any setting. In the hallway. In a restaurant. In our bedroom. On a soccer field. Anywhere we are.

Continually means that any time is the right time to praise God!

>> Adjustment Time

And *continually* means a huge attitude adjustment is in order. *Continually* means that in every moment, we're constantly looking for ways to glorify Him.

Continually gets our worship outside the walls of the church building.

Continually gets our worship outside of our devotional times.

Continually gets worship outside of our camps and youth group times.

Our worship events.

Our MP3 players.

Our headphones.

Continually gets worship into the classroom.

Into our hangout places.

Into our conversations with friends.

Into our Starbucks moments.

Continually gets worship into our entertainment choices.

Our instant messages.

Our hidden thoughts.

Our dark nights.

Our joys.

What God is saying is this: "Everything you are—is Me. Everything you have—is Mine. The life you live is My life that I've freely given you. And I want worshipers who will be constantly reflecting My goodness and grace with that life."

God wants our lives to be a seamless song of worship. God wants our worship to be a way of life.

ADDITIONAL DISCUSSION QUESTIONS

CHAPTER 8: THROUGH JESUS, ALL THE TIME

1. Why is it so important to keep in our minds and hearts the fact that worship is "through Jesus"? Why does it matter? And what does it mean personally for you to do this?

2. In this book's first chapter, we explored the reality that all of us worship all the time (according to the basic, universal meaning of worship). Now as we discover more about the true worship that pleases God, we see Him asking us to worship Him "continually." To offer true worship continually to God, does it help knowing that you're already constantly worshiping anyway?

3. What do you recognize as the most important adjustments needed in your life in order to more continually offer worship to God?

4. Bible passages to explore together: Hebrews 13:15; John 14:6, 15:4–5; Colossians 3:17.

CHAPTER 9: LIPS AND LIVES

Eddy Curry, a twenty-two-year-old professional basketball player with the Chicago Bulls, missed the final month of the 2004–05 regular season and playoffs after experiencing a heart arrhythmia before a March 30 game at Charlotte. He was checked out by a group of Bulls team doctors, but tests ultimately were inconclusive.

One of the doctors, Minneapolis cardiologist Barry Maron, suggested Curry undergo a DNA test to see if he was genetically disposed to hypertrophic cardiomyopathy, a potentially fatal condition. Bulls General Manager John Paxson said if Curry didn't agree to submit to the test, the team might not allow him to suit up.

Curry refused. His representatives pointed out that their client had been cleared to play by his own doctor, a leading cardiologist in Los Angeles, who said a DNA test was unnecessary in this case. They also claimed such tests were unreliable, and that they couldn't rule out any condition definitively.

More important for pro sports—and perhaps society at large—Curry's reps argued that submitting to such a test could set a dangerous precedent. "If employers could give employees DNA tests, then they could find out if there's a propensity for illnesses like cancer, heart disease or alcoholism," Alan Milstein, a lawyer who helped represent Curry, told the *Chicago Tribune*. "They will make personnel decisions based on DNA testing."

Did the Bulls have the right to demand Eddy Curry take a DNA test?

"It's unprecedented," said agent Henry Thomas, speaking for many in the NBA and per-haps all of pro sports. "The ramifications could go well beyond this particular case."[viii]

As a side note: During the writing of this book, Eddy Curry was traded by the Chicago Bulls to the New York Knicks. The Knicks organization tested Curry for any genetic disposition to hypertrophic cardiomyopathy. All tests came back negative.

What if your spiritual DNA were tested? What would it show to be the propensity for your life?

What other youth workers are saying about worship:

—*Worship is living your life for God's glory—shining a light on Him.*

—*Worship is reflecting God's love for me back to Him in all I do.*

LIPS AND LIVES

THE HUGE IDEA:

**EVERYTHING CAN BE WORSHIP
WHEN IT'S DONE FOR GOD'S GLORY.**

JESUS MAKES OUR WORSHIP
ACCEPTABLE TO GOD.

ALL WORSHIP INVOLVES SACRIFICE.

WE WORSHIP GOD FOR WHO
HE IS AND WHAT HE HAS DONE.

WORSHIP STARTS WITH SEEING GOD.

TRUE WORSHIP BEGINS AT
THE CROSS OF CHRIST.

WE NEED TO WORSHIP GOD MORE THAN
GOD NEEDS OUR WORSHIP.

WE ARE MADE TO WORSHIP GOD.

EVERYBODY WORSHIPS SOMETHING.

Our continual sacrifice of praise—

our all-the-time expression of worship to God—
takes two primary shapes. It's made up of words.
And deeds.

Let's look again at that Hebrews passage and see
where it takes us:

> Through Jesus then, let us continually offer
> up a sacrifice of praise to God, that is, the
> fruit of lips that give thanks to His name.
> And do not neglect doing good and sharing,
> for with such sacrifices God is pleased.

The first part of continual praise is the "fruit of
our lips" which magnify God. That phrase "the fruit
of our lips" may sound a little odd, but I like it.

There's no fruit without some kind of root. So
whatever comes out of our mouths actually comes
from the roots that have taken hold deep in our souls.
That is why Scripture says that what comes out of the
mouth is actually coming from the heart (Luke 6:45).

Our praise to God doesn't just roll off our
lips, but springs from deep down inside us. (Very
cool concept!)

THE HUGE IDEA:
EVERYTHING CAN BE
WORSHIP WHEN IT'S DONE
FOR GOD'S GLORY.

Our **praise to God**
doesn't just roll off our lips,
but **springs** from deep down
inside us.

Is your worship mostly "lips" or "life"? How can you change this? Why is it important?

God is looking for people who are always soaking in His Word, sinking roots of His character into their minds and hearts. As a result, true expressions to and about Him are constantly coming out of their mouths.

I think that's what David means when he says, "I will bless the LORD at all times; His praise shall continually be in my mouth" (Psalm 34:1).

>> Actions That Express

But verbal praise isn't the only kind of worship God is into. The passage goes on to expand worship to include acts of compassion and integrity, sacrifices which really make God happy.

Now we're moving beyond the fruit of our lips to consider the fruit of our lives.

And the same principle applies: If we immerse ourselves in God's character, God's character starts to grow "on the limbs of our tree." His character will eventually find expression in the things we do.

For example, when we choose to do what is right in a given situation, God is worshiped. Even if no one else notices or cares, God does. Even if ridicule follows, God is honored. In that moment,

WIRED Idea: Find an enormous tree (preferably near a river or stream) and read Psalm 1. Correlate the root system of the tree to our root system in the character of God. Ask this question: How does one grow strong and deep in God?

God's truth is reflected back to Him. And even if we somehow get penalized for our honesty, God is honored by our sacrifice.

And when we care for someone else, the passage reminds us, then "God is pleased."

It's a lot easier to sing a song than it is to stop and touch the broken. It's a lot less taxing to go to church than to take "church" to your school and to the world. But sharing with others is a sacrifice of worship that makes God smile.

>> What It Can Look Like

I have a friend living in Afghanistan. He's been there for several years, working among some of the most desperate people on earth. Years of war, famine, and evil regimes have reduced their lives to what they wear on their backs.

Men, women, and children—displaced within their own country. No jobs. No home. No shelter. Little future.

My friend is sharp. Educated. And a believer in Christ. John could live anywhere in America. But he doesn't.

WIRED Idea: This may seem like a stretch, but it is so powerful: With parental consent, spend a Sunday morning with your students away from church serving someone else. After you are done, discuss the ramifications of worship in serving. Do you think God smiles on this sort of act of worship? Why or why not? Discuss this statement: God measures the depth of your relationship with Him by your relationships with other people. Agree? Disagree? Why?

Having abandoned the American dream for greater riches, he can be found most days in some Afghan village…overseeing a relief project, establishing an educational training center, or monitoring a food distribution program.

He's loving people and meeting their needs. And when they ask why, John smiles a smile rooted deep down in the grace of God, and he tells them about Jesus Christ.

He is more than a missionary. He's a worshiper in spirit and truth. A worshiper in action and deed.

What do you think moves God more? Us singing "Here I Am To Worship" a hundred more times *Or* one undignified worshiper walking the streets of Afghanistan, touching the world's "least" in Jesus' name.

If you've been playing along, you know by now the answer is BOTH.

The song has a place in the worship of the church, spurring us to lives that are surrendered to Jesus. But at some point we've got to live the song, being willing to go to people everywhere who are waiting to hear about a grace that's free. About a life of purpose.

God loves the world. Every soul in it. He wants all nations to know His name. All people to taste His goodness. Every heart to sing His praise.

But those who have not yet heard of this seeking God will never awaken to worship in truth until we share. Until we worship with our words and our lives. Until we reflect His wonder and grace in every corner of the world.

>> Making the Mundane a Melody

Sure, you're thinking, *going to Afghanistan is a wonderful thing. But I'm just trying to survive tenth grade!*

I understand. Most people are just like you.

No, I don't mean they're sophomores. But most people find themselves in places that don't seem all that spiritual. Or worshipful. Classes that seem pointless apart from logging new information or filling the time. Circumstances that don't appear to have any eternal significance at all.

If you've ever felt like that, I've got great news. You can worship God wherever you are…doing whatever it is you do!

That's the beautiful thing about continual

praise. Your attitude of worship can turn any mundane task into an offering to God.

Worship can even happen at the photocopy machine.

It did for me.

As a college student in Atlanta, I worked part-time at the Centers for Disease Control. Pretty impressive, huh? There I was stemming the spread of infectious diseases, developing groundbreaking technologies to improve life and alleviate human suffering!

Well…not exactly.

To be precise, I was the photocopy boy in the Centers' medical library. My main activity was making photocopies of the hundreds of articles that various doctors wanted for their personal use.

I didn't exactly have an office—more of a cubbyhole. The photocopier was in a four-by-eight-foot room beneath a stairway at the back of the library. The slanted ceiling dropped below head height on one side. The room overflowed with carts loaded with medical journals waiting to be copied, each

CIRCLE THE WORD BIBLE STUDY

(Circle the word that stands out/means most to you and be ready to talk about why you chose that word.)

And whatever you do, in word or deed, do it all in the name of the Lord Jesus, giving thanks to God the Father through him. COLOSSIANS 3:17, NIV having white slips of paper sticking out of them, telling me what to do next.

Hour after hour after hour it was just me and that machine. Day after day the requests piled up. The copying continued.

>> Working, Worshiping

But God was doing a lot in my heart in those days, and the job for me became something more. I'm not trying to overspiritualize what happened (we didn't end up having a revival in the library), but by God's grace I was able to turn that copy room into a place I loved.

For one thing, I wanted to be the best copier on earth, never leaving work until every waiting article was reproduced…something that often required improvements in my technique, speed, and productivity. I would not be denied.

But also, this job gave me lots of time to hang out with God. Photocopying, though manually intensive, doesn't overly deplete the brain. Which left lots of time for thoughts of God. Time to talk to Him. Time to worship. Time to listen. Time to pray.

I think copying medical journals can be (should be) worship. Do you agree? Why/why not? What's the most mundane thing you do? How can you turn it into worship?

Everyone working there knew I was a believer, but they weren't exactly asking me to lead a Bible study or talk about the Savior. My witness was my work…and work was my worship. The way I did my work was possibly even more significant than anything I could do or say.

I became, to put it modestly, the master copier. And you know what? I think the way I did my work reflected something good about the character of God.

When I left, it took three new employees to match my pace! And who knows—one of those articles might have contributed to the untangling of some global disease. (For that, you can thank me later!)

The point is this: Everything on earth (except sin) can be done as an act of worship to God. Everything we do *is* worship when we do it for Him, displaying His face as we go. That, by the way, is why we don't want to sin. Because sin is the one thing that cannot be done in such a way that it brings honor and glory to God. In fact, sin is just the opposite. When we choose to do things our own way, we are saying to God, and the world around us, that our God is not good enough to lead our lives and meet our needs. But everything else besides sin can be turned into worship as we do it in such a way as to reflect His character.

Yep, the way you do your work at school can *and should* be worship.

The way you fry the fries can be, too, as you run the drive-through window at Chick-fil-A.

Your attitude toward your parents can be an act of worship.

Or the way you practice.

Or going out of your way to volunteer at the homeless shelter.

These are all a part of what the verse means when it says, "And do not neglect doing good and sharing, for with such sacrifices God is pleased."

The question is not *what* you do, but *who* you do it for.

Your mission is to turn your place in life into a place of true worship. To do whatever you do in a way that will reflect God's heart to those around you.

Your mission is to worship...with everything you say and all you do.

Give some real life examples of ways you can glorify God (worship Him) outside the walls of the church.

Everything on earth (except sin) **can** be done as an **act of worship to God**.

ADDITIONAL DISCUSSION QUESTIONS

CHAPTER 9: LIPS AND LIVES

1. What specific forms of "doing good" and "sharing with others" has God given you the opportunity and privilege to live out? How have you sensed God's pleasure in this?

2. What does worshiping God mean—or what could it mean—in your own place of work or in school?

3. What needs in the lives of people around you seem most urgent to you? What needs in the world around you tend to weigh down your own heart the most?

4. What specific "sacrifices" do you believe God is calling you to make in your life at this time in order to bring glory to Him and life to people around you?

5. Explore together these Scriptures: Hebrews 13:15–16; 1 Peter 2:5; Philippians 2:12–16.

CHAPTER 10: A PERSONAL PATH TO WORSHIP

On June 25, 2005, emergency workers in London, England, rescued a teenage girl from the arm of a crane some 130 feet above the ground. Emergency services were called to a building site in London after a passerby spotted the fifteen-year-old girl curled up on top of a concrete counterweight high above the ground.

Police and the London Fire Brigade attended to the girl and brought her down in a hydraulic lift after a two-hour rescue. She was taken to the hospital for precautionary checks, and she was later released and went home.

It is believed that the teenager, who has not been named, walked out unnoticed from her home near the site in Dulwich (southeast London), climbed up the crane, and walked across a narrow metal beam to her perch on the counterweight.

Why, you ask?

She was sleepwalking.[ix]

Strange and mind-boggling to think that a teenager could sleepwalk her way onto the arm of a crane some 130 feet above the ground, isn't it? But what is as strange, if not more, is the fact that so many people sleepwalk their way through life, finding themselves in perilous predicaments and circumstances, asleep to their reason for existence.

Are you sleepwalking through life?

What other youth workers are saying about worship:

—Worship is living your life for God's glory—shining a light on Him.

—Worship is reflecting God's love for me back to Him in all I do.

A PERSONAL PATH TO WORSHIP

THE HUGE IDEA:

KNOWING GOD FUELS OUR WORSHIP.

EVERYTHING CAN BE WORSHIP
WHEN IT'S DONE FOR GOD'S GLORY.

JESUS MAKES OUR WORSHIP
ACCEPTABLE TO GOD.

ALL WORSHIP INVOLVES SACRIFICE.

WE WORSHIP GOD FOR WHO
HE IS AND WHAT HE HAS DONE.

WORSHIP STARTS WITH SEEING GOD.

TRUE WORSHIP BEGINS AT
THE CROSS OF CHRIST.

WE NEED TO WORSHIP GOD MORE THAN
GOD NEEDS OUR WORSHIP.

WE ARE MADE TO WORSHIP GOD.

EVERYBODY WORSHIPS SOMETHING.

Developing a personal life of worship is the

most important thing you can do. It's where the worship journey begins.

We've talked a lot about our worship being a response to God. If that's so, we've got to keep Him in view, daily pursuing the process of discovering who He is.

For some, I know, that's an intimidating task. *Get to know God?* you wonder. *Where would I even start?*

Slowly. Simply.

You take one step at a time.

>> Big Things, in Small Pieces

The first (and so far only!) real mountain I've climbed is the Matterhorn. No, not the one at Disney! The nearly 15,000-foot version in the Alps—a sheer triangle of snow-covered rock looming above the pristine little village of Zermatt, Switzerland.

Though at home I'd trained like crazy in the summer heat, I hadn't taken the time to actually

THE HUGE IDEA:

KNOWING GOD

FUELS OUR WORSHIP.

learn about the mountain itself. I'd never even seen a picture of the mountain before. My friend and fellow climber, Marc, had assured me it was doable. That's all I needed to know.

When we arrived in Zermatt, what I saw at the valley's end was an intimidating peak of stone. The two angled sides facing the village seemed to rise straight up to a narrow ridgeline top. Certainly no one was going up that way!

At first sight of it, I said to my wife, Shelley, "Don't worry; our way up must be on the back side. There's no way we're climbing that!"

Well, to make a really long and death-defying story short, we did. We climbed right up that imposing face!

This was more mountain than I bargained for, and I was quickly aware of the fact that I hadn't trained hard enough or well enough. I instantly wished I'd done a little investigating before we arrived. Yet, had I done so, we most likely wouldn't have arrived at all!

In fact, on the main Matterhorn web page, which I didn't check out until we were safely home, is the disclaimer, "Inexperienced climbers should not attempt an ascent of the Matterhorn as their first mountain."

As it turns out, the Matterhorn is one of Europe's toughest climbs, with one of the highest death rates for climbers. It wasn't scaled until 1865—even way back then it was the last of the Alps to surrender to exploration.

That imposing face of granite was swimming in my head as Marc and I tried to sleep high upon the mountain at the Hornli Hut.

Honestly, I had my doubts about the climb.

But we set out for the summit sprint in the early morning darkness—along with our two Swiss guides—and were soon going straight up what seemed like mile-high slabs of unconquerable granite. We climbed for the most part on our hands and feet. And we did it in little chunks—constantly moving, yet only a few feet at a time.

At last, we stood on the eighteen-inch-wide summit of this mountaineering jewel. I wept both tears of relief and tears of amazement. Even more impressive, we made it back down again; an

To **draw near to God** simply means to take the **first step** towards Him **today**.

achievement that I now know is far more demanding (and important) than getting to the top. But that's another story.

>> Climbing Mount God

So—how do you scale something as majestic as Mount God? How do you get to know someone as big as Him?

Answer: a little at a time.

We don't wake up one day to discover that we are really "tight" with God just because we want to be. Knowing God—like going up the Matterhorn—requires that we pay a price. And that we take a lot of small steps every day.

But the main thing is to take the first step. In the little book of James we find the promise, "Draw near to God and He will draw near to you." God has already made the first move, inviting you through His Son Jesus Christ to come as close as you want. But you have to respond, telling (and showing) God that you want to be His friend.

To *draw near to God* simply means to take the first step towards Him today. How? A good place to

WIRED Idea: If you live in a mountainous region, take your students on a hike to the top of a mountain. If you do not, search your town or city for a rock climbing wall and have a blast. Use these experiences as a way to dialogue about the process of climbing something so large. Parallel this idea with God. Have students journal their thoughts.

start is with this prayer: *God, I want to know you!*
Don't just pray the prayer, really tell God that's what
you want most from Him. Ask Him to open your
eyes, expand your ability to know and discover who
He is, and draw close to you as you run to Him.

At some point you're going to have to carve out
some "alone time." With God. Some people call
this a quiet time, others a devotion time. But whatever you call it, you are going to need some space
that is for you and God alone. Once there, open
His Word (after all, it is God's autobiography) and
as you read look for Him more than information
about Him. Talk to Him as you read His words,
thanking Him for who He is and all He has done in
your life.

Lay your cares in His hands and ask Him to
teach you how to reflect Christ more clearly in
your life.

What may be even more important than your
time alone with Him is that you walk away from
that time fully aware that He is with you, wanting
to be a part of everything you do. Don't make the
mistake of spending fifteen minutes alone with God

How difficult is it for you to worship when you're alone with God? What kind of barriers do you typically face? What can help you overcome them?

only to forget about Him for the other twenty-three hours and forty-five minutes of the day.

In every little step you take throughout the day, keep Him in view. Talk to Him all day long, including Him in everything you do.

When I was in high school I played tennis all the time. I'd practice almost every day after school and then sometimes go home and hit against a wall by myself at night. Those were some of my favorite times with God. Yep. I'd talk and hang out with God the whole time, just me and Him together enjoying life.

>> Little Pieces of a Massive God

But to worship Him best we have to know Him well. A good place to begin is by flipping this book over to the "30-Day Worship Journey" and carving out a few quiet minutes every day for a month. It's been said that doing anything (good or bad) for thirty days helps form a habit in our hearts. So give it a thirty-day shot as you seek to climb higher in your relationship with God.

Before you begin each day, breathe this simple

prayer to God: "Father, I'm here for You. Please show me who You are."

Open to the Psalms and begin to read. The goal here is quality, not quantity. You may be content with a verse or two, or you may want to focus on a whole Psalm. But don't speed along. Let the words sink in.

As you read, look for one attribute of God that seems to grab your attention. An attribute is simply something that's true about God. A part of His character. A facet of His heart. One of His names.

Maybe you'll be drawn to His mercy. Or His consistency. His love. His holiness.

Maybe your heart will zero in on the fact that He's your Sustainer. Shepherd. Shelter. Friend.

When you feel like one thing has captured your heart, write that attribute on the top of your journal page. You might want to write the verse down, too.

Now take some time to meditate on that aspect of God's character. For example, think about what it means that God is wise. That He embodies "all the treasures of wisdom and knowledge" (Colossians

2:3). And think about what God's wisdom means to your life today.

After a few minutes, write your thoughts to God. You might write your own psalm of praise back to Him, or just a stream of thoughts as they spill over from your heart to His.

You might write a new song, or just sing one you already know that magnifies the dimension of His heart that you're focusing on.

Make it personal. Intimate. Honest.

Remember, there's no right or wrong way to journal your response to what you see of Him. Two sentences can be as powerful as two pages.

Now carry that word with you all day long. Keep the conversation with God going everywhere you go.

You might be surprised how many times that characteristic surfaces as you walk through your day.

Every time it does, thank Him for the truth that He has shown you. Praise Him for who He is.

CIRCLE THE WORD BIBLE STUDY

(Circle the word that stands out/means most to you and be ready to talk about why you chose that word.)

I have set the LORD always before me. Because he is at my right hand, I will not be shaken. Therefore my heart is glad and my tongue rejoices; my body also will rest secure. PSALM 16:8-9, NIV

After thirty days, you'll be encouraged at how far along you are on the path of knowing Him. And you'll be amazed at how much more there is of Him to explore.

>> Getting Closer Is the Key

I don't guess you'd be too surprised to know I have a huge print of the Matterhorn hanging on my office wall. And a large edition coffee-table book about the mountain is at my house.

More than one unsuspecting visitor to our home has been subjected to my tales about the climb, as section by section this book records the very route of our ascent in full-page photos that take your breath away.

When I first picked up the book in a shop in Zermatt, I was totally unnerved by the immensity of the images. Then, as I looked more closely at what I first thought were shots of the mountain alone, I could see antlike men, climbers within the rocks. Barely visible dots making their way slowly up the mountain. The closer I looked, the more little people I found.

WIRED Idea: Guide your students through how to use the 30-Day Worship Journey. It is really important that they grasp how to use a journal, so spend some time walking them through a few days.

Go ahead and flip your book over and start your 30-Day Worship Journey.

"Over there, three more. And look right here, six more going up."

I discovered this giant rock is a little deceiving. From a distance the Matterhorn looks smooth and sheer. But once you actually get on the mountain you discover it's jagged. Full of cracks and crevices. Little places to get a foothold, or a toehold, as you make your way to its peak.

In the same way, there are endless crevices in the character of God. When we break His Word into little chunks, we find a lot of places to settle. Hidden places, offering good footing as we seek to know Him more.

ADDITIONAL DISCUSSION QUESTIONS

CHAPTER 10: A PERSONAL PATH TO WORSHIP

1. Talk about one or two facets of God's character that have meant the most to you in recent days. How did these come to your attention? How have you grown in your understanding of God?

2. What helps you most to sense that you're drawing close to God?

3. Bible passages to explore together: John 1:18; 2 Corinthians 4:6; Psalm 27:8, 67:1–2.

CHAPTER 11: MOVING BEYOND ME, TO US

The story is told about a Special Olympics footrace a few years ago. Nine contestants, all physically or mentally challenged, assembled at the starting line for the one-hundred-yard dash. At the gun, they all started out, not exactly in a dash, but with relish to run the race to the finish and win. All, that is, except one little boy who stumbled on the asphalt, tumbled over a couple of times, and began to cry. The other eight heard the boy cry. They slowed down and looked back. Then several turned around and went back. One girl with Down's syndrome bent down and kissed him and said, "This will make it better." They linked arms with the fallen runner and walked together to the finish line.

What other youth workers are saying about worship:

—*Worship is a choice to amplify the God of gods.*

—*Worship is utilizing all God has entrusted you with in whatever you do to honor and glorify God!*

MOVING BEYOND ME, TO US

THE HUGE IDEA:

UNIFIED VOICES
MAKE THE LOUDEST SONG.

KNOWING GOD FUELS OUR WORSHIP.

EVERYTHING CAN BE WORSHIP
WHEN IT'S DONE FOR GOD'S GLORY.

JESUS MAKES OUR WORSHIP
ACCEPTABLE TO GOD.

ALL WORSHIP INVOLVES SACRIFICE.

WE WORSHIP GOD FOR WHO
HE IS AND WHAT HE HAS DONE.

WORSHIP STARTS WITH SEEING GOD.

TRUE WORSHIP BEGINS AT
THE CROSS OF CHRIST.

WE NEED TO WORSHIP GOD MORE THAN
GOD NEEDS OUR WORSHIP.

WE ARE MADE TO WORSHIP GOD.

EVERYBODY WORSHIPS SOMETHING.

Worship is a personal thing.

But it's also something we do together.

In other words, our responses of worship to God are both personal and corporate. And each kind of response is intertwined with the other.

That's why we say:

Worship is…

our response,
both personal and corporate,
to God—
for who He is!
and what He has done!
expressed in and by the things we say
and the way we live.

Christianity is not an individual sport so much as it is a family deal. Through Christ we've been reconnected to God, and in Him we're linked to

THE HUGE IDEA:
UNIFIED VOICES MAKE
THE LOUDEST SONG.

We **aren't** designed to operate on a **weekly worship cycle**…

…but on a **moment-by-moment** connection of **personal worship** that's as much a part of our lives as the **air we breathe**.

each other. We're His body. His people. His family.

Each one of us plays a unique role. We fit with the body in a necessary way.

I'm not talking about joining organized religion, but the organism called the church. If you're a believer in God, He has made you a part of His body, His people. It's really not your call, but His. He has already made you a member. And a part of your worship is to make a connection with other believers around you.

The primary purpose of the church (the people of God) is worship. At its core, the church exists to glorify God. And, without your life and voice, the body's expression is incomplete.

But even in the corporate setting, worship doesn't begin with a group activity. It begins with our individual responses to what God has revealed to us about Himself. Those responses don't just happen once a week…they happen day by day.

We aren't designed to operate on a weekly worship cycle, but on a moment-by-moment connection of personal worship that's as much a part of our lives as the air we breathe. It's how we're wired.

WIRED Idea: Have students spend one week meditating on this phrase and then acting on its intent: Come to church worshiping.

Ask how acting on this concept changed their worship experience. Discuss how this idea differs from what most are conditioned to consider as it relates to worship.

>> Putting It All Together

As we come together with other believers in worship, we can bring that same sense of focus we've had in our daily journey. We bring that same determined devotion.

Most of my life, I thought that you went to church to worship. But now I see that the better approach is to go worshiping to church.

Trust me, church is a lot better when our gatherings are filled with people who have been pursuing God for six days before they get there. Church as a "refill" or a "tank-up" is a disaster. Corporate worship works best when we arrive with something to offer God. As opposed to only coming to get something for ourselves from God.

Church is supposed to be a celebration of our personal journeys with God since we were last together.

Imagine what would happen if each person in the congregation was seeking the face of God throughout the week. Some would encounter sorrow, others major happiness. But all would have a story to tell of God's faithfulness in good times and bad.

Most of my life, I thought that you **went to church to worship.** But now I see that the better approach is to **go worshiping to church.**

What would happen if we came worshiping to church, filled with an awareness of His presence before we even reached the door? Well, for one, the lead worshiper's job would be a lot easier! And the intensity of our collective offering would be full-on.

Can you see it? All of our personal streams of worship flowing into one surging river. One mighty anthem. A beautiful mosaic, telling an even greater story of who God is and what He's done.

People leave a gathering like that inspired to seek Him as never before. And they come back again bringing worship with them, starting the cycle all over again.

The worship circle is complete. Unbroken.

>> Connecting the Dots

We need to overhaul the way we view the Sunday service. Or whenever it is we meet together with others to worship.

Usually no one has given the service a moment's thought until they arrive. We come through the door like we're stopping at the mall. We sit and chat. We wait for someone to guide us before we ever stop and connect with the privilege of it all.

Yet the corporate gathering is a sacred thing. A special thing. A holy thing. Maybe we need bigger buildings after all. Cathedrals that remind us that we're really small and God is really big. Buildings that force us to look up.

Bruce Leafblad, one of the major shapers of my perspective on worship, has a great definition of worship. Part of it goes like this: "Worship is centering our mind's attention and our heart's affection on the Lord."[3]

You can't make it any more clear than that.

True worship requires our attention. I know that's difficult in our commercial-driven culture, where our television-trained minds have geared us for a break every seven minutes. But God requires us to love Him with all our minds. His sheer immensity and beauty demands our complete attention.

Have you ever been talking with somebody who was constantly looking around while they were talking to you, checking out the scene while you tried to make your point? It makes you just want to walk away, doesn't it?

In my late teens I used to often sit alone in the worship service so I could concentrate on God without being distracted (or distracting someone else). What are practical ways you can be more attentive in corporate worship?

Why do we think it's any different with God?

When we come to worship together it's imperative that we find God and lock our gaze with His. That's not easy with all the other people in the room. But our primary reason for being there is to see Him. At least it should be.

I don't know about you, but my attention wanders like crazy. For me, the corporate worship experience is a constant "roundup," me chasing down my drifting thoughts and reattaching them to God. So I'm not saying it's easy to stay focused on Him. Just that it's essential.

>> Face-to-Face, Eye-to-Eye

As we worship with others, it's important that we find Him, because our attention aims our affection.

We have the amazing potential to shoot arrows of affection into the heart of God. If those arrows are going to hit the target, we have to know where the target is.

And if those arrows from our hearts are going to register with His, they have to be honest and true.

That means we have to think carefully about what we're saying…what we're singing. And who we're singing to. Sometimes we would be better off saying nothing than standing there lying to the face of God. Our worship would honor Him more if we just stopped singing and realigned our heart with His.

I believe for this to happen, we have to connect with God before we arrive. Worship is an intentional thing. It's something we set our hearts to do. So the next time you come to worship with other believers, take a deep breath as you cross the parking lot. Think about the vastness of the God you are coming to meet. Think about His love and grace as you pass through the doors.

And before the worship service begins, begin to worship in your heart.

The key is to come prepared. To come worshiping. To connect with God. To keep your eyes on Him.

As we conclude the discussion of this book, what do you most want to tell God about the life of worship you desire to live? Talk openly about this before you pray together and actually express those desires to your loving Father in heaven.

>> Worship Is So Much More

You are a worshiper. It's what you do. And you *are* going to worship—no matter what! That's the simple truth of this little book.

Something's going to grab your affection. Someone is going to captivate your heart and mind. One thing is going to rise to the surface of your values and drive your life, aiming your steps and determining your destiny.

The invitation of God has come to you, inviting you to join those who glorify Him with all of who they are. He's inviting you to discover His infinite worth, giving you the privilege of exalting Him as infinitely worthy.

Through Christ, you can breathe again, inhaling the wonder of God that always surrounds you, exhaling words and deeds of praise that reflect all of who He is.

So, whether personal or corporate, let's make this what we do. Let's give Him all we are.

WIRED Idea: Attend a worship experience with the entire purpose being to practice aiming your mind's attention and heart's affection on God. Discuss what makes this so difficult. What are some things that make doing this more successful?

At the beginning of this book, and again before chapter four, you wrote out your definition of worship. Without looking back at those, write one final definition for worship below.

[

]

How has this changed—or has it changed—from when you first started WIRED?

[

]

ADDITIONAL DISCUSSION QUESTIONS

CHAPTER 11: MOVING BEYOND ME, TO US

1. This chapter talks about the need to "go worshiping to church." Is this something you experience in your life? What makes it harder (or easier) for you to come worshiping to church?

2. When do you think it might be appropriate in a corporate worship setting to be silent and not join in with others who are singing and praising God together?

3. How can we keep from being more interested in our experiences of worship than we are in experiencing God Himself?

4. This chapter paints a picture of a congregation that truly seeks God during the week before coming together on Sunday. To what degree is this already happening in your church? What can help cause it to happen more and more?

5. Explore together these Scriptures: Isaiah 26:8; Psalm 33:1–5; 34:3; 148; Revelation 4:11; 5:12.

NOTES

1. The phrase "the wonderful cross" is used in a Chris Tomlin adaptation of the classic worship song "When I Survey the Wondrous Cross" (Isaac Watts, 1707; adaptation by Chris Tomlin in *The Noise We Make*, Six Steps Records/Sparrow Records, 2001).

2. Louie Giglio, 2001.

3. Bruce Leafblad's definition in full (as given in his course "Introduction to Church Music" at Southwestern Baptist Theological Seminary, 1983): "Worship is communion with God in which believers, by grace, center their mind's attention and their heart's affection on the Lord, humbly glorifying God in response to His greatness and His Word."

i. Freda Parker, "The Pantheon—Rome—126 AD: A temple to all gods," Monolithic Dome Institute. http://www.monolithic.com/thedome/pantheon/ (accessed November 10, 2005).

ii. Michelle Healy, "Disk of Stars Found Around Black Hole," USA Today, September 21, 2005.

iii. Warren St. John, *Rammer Jammer Yellow Hammer: A Journey into the Heart of Fan Mania* (New York: Crown Publishers, 2004), 11–12.

iv. Paul Barman, "Superpowers: A Scientific Probe!" *Wired*, September 2005. http://www.wired.com/wired/archive/13.09/play.html?pg=5 (accessed November 15, 2005).

v. Reuters, "N.M. Officer Uses Helicopter for Food Run," *USA Today*, October 9, 2001.

vi. Malcolm Gladwell, *The Tipping Point* (New York: Little, Brown and Company, 2000), 30–34.

vii. Steven D. Levitt and Stephen J. Dubner, *Freakonomics: A Rogue Economist Explores the Hidden Side of Everything* (New York: William Morrow, 2005), 149–150.

viii. Marty Burns, "In Whose Best Interests?" SI.com, September 29, 2005. http://sportsillustrated.cnn.com/2005/writers/marty_burns/09/28/curry/ (accessed November 15, 2005).

ix. Reuters, "Sleepwalker rescued from crane," CNN.com, 2005. http://www.cnn.com/2005/WORLD/europe/07/06/crane.rescue.reut/index.html?section=cnn_topstories

Credits/Thanks:

Jennifer Hill, Production Coordinator, Creative Input
Stuart Hall, Wired Connections, Wired Ideas
Deeann Carson, Creation of art pages for 30 Day Journey
The Multnomah Team

WIRED: FOR A LIFE OF WORSHIP

is the student edition of *The Air I Breathe.* Revised and expanded edition available July 2006.

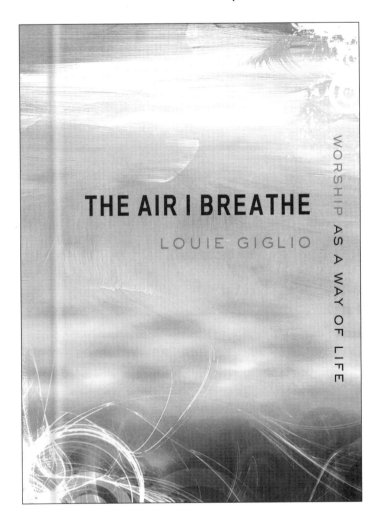

THE AIR I BREATHE

LOUIE GIGLIO

WORSHIP AS A WAY OF LIFE

The Air I Breathe

ISBN: 1-59052-670-8
Price: US $12.99

Get all the latest on Passion Conferences
and hear Louie's talks at

268Generation.com

DAY 30

READ & MEDITATE:

READ & MEDITATE:

DAY 28

READ & MEDITATE:

READ & MEDITATE:

READ & MEDITATE:

READ & MEDITATE:

CONGRATULATIONS. YOU ARE OVER HALFWAY

to the thirty-day mark and you're doing great. Think about it. If someone asks you to tell them about God, you have twenty things you could tell them about Him. Very cool.

For the next ten days you get to choose your own Psalm or other passage of Scripture to dive into. Once you've found your passage, write the key verses from that passage on the left page of the *Journey*. Once you have the key passage written in the *Journey*, circle the attributes of God that you see. Choose one for the day, and go for it.

Here are some Psalms to choose from for the next ten days, or you can find your own to explore…

¹ The LORD is my shepherd, I shall not be in want.

² He makes me lie down in green pastures,

he leads me beside quiet waters,

³ he restores my soul.

He guides me in paths of righteousness

for his name's sake.

⁴ Even though I walk

through the valley of the shadow of death,

I will fear no evil, for you are with me;

your rod and your staff, they comfort me.

⁵ You prepare a table before me

in the presence of my enemies.

You anoint my head with oil;

my cup overflows.

⁵ Surely goodness and love will follow me

all the days of my life,

and I will dwell in the house of the LORD forever.

[7] I will praise the LORD , who counsels me;

even at night my heart instructs me.

[8] I have set the LORD always before me.

Because he is at my right hand, I will not be shaken.

[9] Therefore my heart is glad and my tongue rejoices;

my body also will rest secure,

[10] because you will not abandon me to the grave,

nor will you let your Holy One see decay.

[11] You have made known to me the path of life;

you will fill me with joy in your presence,

with eternal pleasures at your right hand.

¹¹ If I say, "Surely the darkness will hide me
and the light become night around me,"

¹² even the darkness will not be dark to you;
the night will shine like the day,
for darkness is as light to you.

¹³ For you created my inmost being;
you knit me together in my mother's womb.

¹⁴ I praise you because I am fearfully and wonderfully made;
your works are wonderful,
I know that full well.

¹⁵ My frame was not hidden from you
when I was made in the secret place.
When I was woven together in the depths of the earth,

¹⁶ your eyes saw my unformed body.
All the days ordained for me
were written in your book
before one of them came to be.

¹⁷ How precious to me are your thoughts, O God!
How vast is the sum of them!

¹⁸ Were I to count them,
they would outnumber the grains of sand.

When I awake,
I am still with you

¹ How long, O LORD ? Will you forget me forever?

How long will you hide your face from me?

² How long must I wrestle with my thoughts

and every day have sorrow in my heart?

How long will my enemy triumph over me?

³ Look on me and answer, O LORD my God.

Give light to my eyes, or I will sleep in death;

⁴ my enemy will say, "I have overcome him,"

and my foes will rejoice when I fall.

⁵ But I trust in your unfailing love;

my heart rejoices in your salvation.

⁶ I will sing to the LORD ,

for he has been good to me.

¹ In you, O L ORD , I have taken refuge;
let me never be put to shame;
deliver me in your righteousness.

² Turn your ear to me,
come quickly to my rescue;

be my rock of refuge,
a strong fortress to save me.

³ Since you are my rock and my fortress,
for the sake of your name lead and guide me.

⁴ Free me from the trap that is set for me,
for you are my refuge.

⁵ Into your hands I commit my spirit;
redeem me, O L ORD , the God of truth.

⁶ I hate those who cling to worthless idols;
I trust in the L ORD .

⁷ I will be glad and rejoice in your love,
for you saw my affliction
and knew the anguish of my soul.

⁸ You have not handed me over to the enemy
but have set my feet in a spacious place.

¹ The LORD is my light and my salvation—
whom shall I fear?

The LORD is the stronghold of my life—
of whom shall I be afraid?

² When evil men advance against me
to devour my flesh,

when my enemies and my foes attack me,
they will stumble and fall.

³ Though an army besiege me,
my heart will not fear;

though war break out against me,
even then will I be confident.

⁴ One thing I ask of the LORD ,
this is what I seek:

that I may dwell in the house of the LORD
all the days of my life,

to gaze upon the beauty of the LORD
and to seek him in his temple.

⁵ For in the day of trouble
he will keep me safe in his dwelling;

he will hide me in the shelter of his tabernacle
and set me high upon a rock.

⁶ Then my head will be exalted
above the enemies who surround me;

at his tabernacle will I sacrifice with shouts of joy;
I will sing and make music to the LORD .

⁷ Hear my voice when I call, O LORD ;
be merciful to me and answer me.

⁸ My heart says of you, "Seek his face!"
Your face, LORD , I will seek.

⁹ Do not hide your face from me,
do not turn your servant away in anger;
you have been my helper.

Do not reject me or forsake me,
O God my Savior.

¹⁰ Though my father and mother forsake me,
the LORD will receive me.

¹ Praise the LORD , O my soul;

all my inmost being, praise his holy name.

² Praise the LORD , O my soul,

and forget not all his benefits-

³ who forgives all your sins

and heals all your diseases,

⁴ who redeems your life from the pit

and crowns you with love and compassion,

⁵ who satisfies your desires with good things

so that your youth is renewed like the eagle's.

⁶ The LORD works righteousness

and justice for all the oppressed.

⁷ He made known his ways to Moses,

his deeds to the people of Israel:

⁸ The LORD is compassionate and gracious,

slow to anger, abounding in love.

¹ I will praise you, O LORD , with all my heart;
before the "gods" I will sing your praise.

² I will bow down toward your holy temple
and will praise your name
for your love and your faithfulness,

for you have exalted above all things
your name and your word.

³ When I called, you answered me;
you made me bold and stouthearted.

⁴ May all the kings of the earth praise you, O LORD ,
when they hear the words of your mouth.

⁵ May they sing of the ways of the LORD ,
for the glory of the LORD is great.

⁶ Though the LORD is on high, he looks upon the lowly,
but the proud he knows from afar.

⁷ Though I walk in the midst of trouble,
you preserve my life;

you stretch out your hand against the anger of my foes,
with your right hand you save me.

⁸ The LORD will fulfill his purpose for me;
your love, O LORD , endures forever—
do not abandon the works of your hands.

7 The law of the LORD is perfect,

reviving the soul.

The statutes of the LORD are trustworthy,

making wise the simple.

8 The precepts of the LORD are right,

giving joy to the heart.

The commands of the LORD are radiant,

giving light to the eyes.

9 The fear of the LORD is pure,

enduring forever.

The ordinances of the LORD are sure

and altogether righteous.

10 They are more precious than gold,

than much pure gold;

they are sweeter than honey,

than honey from the comb.

[1] How lovely is your dwelling place,

O LORD Almighty!

[2] My soul yearns even faints,

for the courts of the LORD ;

my heart and my flesh cry out

for the living God.

[3] Even the sparrow has found a home,

and the swallow a nest for herself,

where she may have her young—

 a place near your altar, O LORD Almighty, my King and my God.

[4] Blessed are those who dwell in your house;

they are ever praising you.

[5] Blessed are those whose strength is in you,

who have set their hearts on pilgrimage.

YOU MADE IT THIS FAR; WAY TO GO.

Ten days down and we are getting to know God a little better every day. As you continue, remember that the goal is not to fill in the space on the page, but to know God and worship Him. Before you begin each day from here on out, whisper this prayer to Him. "God, I want to know you more. Please continue to open my eyes and show me who You are. I am here for You."

Now that you have the hang of it, we are going to let you circle and highlight the attributes of God you see in the selected passage. Find as many as you can, then as you read and meditate on the passage, let one of those attributes rise to the top of your list. Once it does, choose that attribute for the day and write it on the righthand page. After that, you know what to do.

Unrivaled

Reigning

¹ The Lord reigns, let the earth be glad;

let the distant shores rejoice. — Joy giver

Solid

fair

² Clouds and thick darkness surround him;

righteousness and justice are the foundation of his throne.

Victorious   Enthroned

³ Fire goes before him

and consumes his foes on every side.

Light

⁴ His lightning lights up the world;   Awe-inspiring

the earth sees and trembles.

⁵ The mountains melt like wax before the Lord ,

before the Lord of all the earth. — Ruler

Righteousness

⁶ The heavens proclaim his righteousness,

and all the peoples see his glory.

Famous

⁷ All who worship images are put to shame,

those who boast in idols—

worship him, all you gods!

Unrivaled

Dependable

Active

Loyal   Honorable

7 The works of his hands are faithful and just;

all his precepts are trustworthy.

Dependable

Steadfast

8 They are steadfast for ever and ever, ——— Timeless

done in faithfulness and uprightness.

Upright

Faithful

Redemptive

9 He provided redemption for his people;

he ordained his covenant forever—

Holy

Covenant Keeper

holy and awesome is his name.

Respected

Awesome Beginnging Wise

10 The fear of the Lord is the beginning of wisdom;

all who follow his precepts have good understanding.

To him belongs eternal praise.

Forever Praised

Shelter

Listening

¹ Hear my cry, O God;

listen to my prayer.

Omnipresent-Everywhere

² From the ends of the earth I call to you,

Leader

I call as my heart grows faint;

High

lead me to the rock that is higher than I.

Refuge

³ For you have been my refuge,

a strong tower against the foe.

Fortress

Protector

⁴ I long to dwell in your tent forever

Dwelling

and take refuge in the shelter of your wings.

Hearing

Shelter

⁵ For you have heard my vows, O God;

you have given me the heritage of those who fear your name.

Reverenced

Defender

¹ O Lᴏʀᴅ , how many are my foes!

How many rise up against me!

² Many are saying of me,

"God will not deliver him."

Defender

Surrounding

³ But you are a shield around me, O Lord ;

you bestow glory on me and lift up my head.

Help

Hope

⁴ To the Lᴏʀᴅ I cry aloud,

and he answers me from his holy hill.

Rest giver

Responder

⁵ I lie down and sleep;

I wake again, because the Lord sustains me.

Confidence

Sustainer

⁶ I will not fear the tens of thousands

drawn up against me on every side.

Liberator

⁷ Arise, O Lᴏʀᴅ !

Deliver me , O my God!

Warrior

Strike all my enemies on the jaw;

break the teeth of the wicked.

Deliverer

⁸ From the Lᴏʀᴅ comes deliverance.

May your blessing be on your people.

Faithful

Worshipped by all

Praised

¹ Shout for joy to the LORD , all the earth.

² Worship the Lord with gladness;

come before him with joyful songs.

God
Owner

Maker

³ Know that the Lord is God.

Shepherd

It is he who made us, and we are his;

we are his people, the sheep of his pasture.

⁴ Enter his gates with thanksgiving   Praiseworthy

and his courts with praise;

give thanks to him and praise his name.

Unchanging

Good

⁵ For the Lord is good and his love endures forever;

his faithfulness continues through all generations.

Faithful

Never ending

Generous

Reigning King

Unending

Enduring

Faithful

Promise Keeper

Sustainer

Maker

Lifter

Provider

Generous

Satisfy

Perfect

Available

Loving

[13] Your kingdom is an everlasting kingdom,

and your dominion endures through all generations.

The Lord is faithful to all his promises

and loving toward all he has made .

[14] The LORD upholds all those who fall

and lifts up all who are bowed down.

[15] The eyes of all look to you,

and you give them their food at the proper time.

[16] You open your hand

and satisfy the desires of every living thing.

[17] The Lord is righteous in all his ways

and loving toward all he has made.

[18] The LORD is near to all who call on him,

to all who call on him in truth.

Supreme

¹ Sing to the LORD a new song;

sing to the LORD , all the earth.

² Sing to the LORD , praise his name;

proclaim his salvation day after day.

Savior ———————————————————— Glorious

³ Declare his glory among the nations,

his marvelous deeds among all peoples.

Great ————————

⁴ For great is the Lord and most worthy of praise;

he is to be feared above all gods. ———— Supreme

⁵ For all the gods of the nations are idols,

but the Lord made the heavens.————Creator

Majestic ————

⁶ Splendor and majesty are before him;

strength and glory are in his sanctuary.

Strong

Forgiving

[1] Out of the depths I cry to you, O LORD ;

Everywhere

[2] O Lord, hear my voice.

Attentive

Let your ears be attentive

to my cry for mercy. *Mercy*

[3] If you, O LORD , kept a record of sins,

O Lord, who could stand?

Forgiving

[4] But with you there is forgiveness;

therefore you are feared.

Longed for

[5] I wait for the LORD , my soul waits,

and in his word I put my hope.

Hope

[6] My soul waits for the Lord

more than watchmen wait for the morning,

more than watchmen wait for the morning.

[7] O Israel, put your hope in the LORD ,

for with the LORD is unfailing love

and with him is full redemption.

Unfailing Love

[8] He himself will redeem Israel

from all their sins. *Sin-stain remover*

Refuge

Exalted

Praiseworthy

Lord of all

Responsive

Liberator

Accessible to everyone

Redeemer

Deliverer

Satisfying

Refuge

[1] I will extol the LORD at all times;

his praise will always be on my lips.

[2] My soul will boast in the LORD ;

let the afflicted hear and rejoice.

[3] Glorify the Lord with me;

let us exalt his name together.

[4] I sought the LORD , and he answered me;

he delivered me from all my fears.

[5] Those who look to him are radiant;

their faces are never covered with shame.

[6] This poor man called,

and the LORD heard him;

he saved him out of all his troubles.

[7] The angel of the LORD encamps around those who fear him,

and he delivers them.

[8] Taste and see that the LORD is good;

blessed is the man who takes refuge in him

Creator

¹ Sing joyfully to the LORD , you righteous;

it is fitting for the upright to praise him.

² Praise the LORD with the harp;

make music to him on the ten-stringed lyre.

³ Sing to him a new song; — *Music lover*

play skillfully, and shout for joy.

⁴ For the word of the Lord is right and true;

he is faithful in all he does. *Truth*

⁵ The LORD loves righteousness and justice; *Lover*

the earth is full of his unfailing love .

⁶ By the word of the LORD were the heavens made,

their starry host by the breath of his mouth.

Huge *Creator*

⁷ He gathers the waters of the sea into jars;

he puts the deep into storehouses.

Feared

⁸ Let all the earth fear the Lord ;

let all the people of the world revere him.

Revered

⁹ For he spoke, and it came to be;

he commanded, and it stood firm. *Originator*

Mine (My God)

Father, I am amazed today that as great as You are I can call You mine. It's not that You belong to me — not that You do whatever I tell You — but that You are mine. You made the world and everything I see (not to mention all the stuff I can't see), but You know my name and have allowed me to call You Father.

I guess when I think about it everybody around me has some kind of god, something they believe in and something that determines how they live their lives. But I am so glad I have You.

You rescued me when I had no hope.
You pulled me up from the mess I made of my life.
You came when I cried out to You. You always do.
You, God, cleaned me up and washed me off.
    Thank You Jesus.
You put my feet on solid ground.
God, You are my solid ground.
And You allowed me to worship You.
You gave me a new song, not the same old song the world
    is singing.
My song is a song of praise to You because You deserve it.
    You are worthy.
And the stuff You have planned for my life... wow!
There's no way I could know all the amazing plans You have for me,
but I love what You have done so far.
And to top it all off, I belong to You and You belong to me.

I like saying to You today what David wrote in this Psalm,
"O Lord, my God." I want You to be the God of me and
I want to be Wholly Yours today.

Thank You for being mine.
Amen.

That's how simple it is. God reveals something about Himself, and you respond in worship. Ready? Let the journey begin.

Rescuing

Listening

¹I waited patiently for the LORD;

he turned to me and heard my cry.

²He lifted me out of the slimy pit,

out of the mud and mire;

he set my feet on a rock

Restoring

and gave me a firm place to stand.

³He put a new song in my mouth,

a hymn of praise to our God.

Many will see and fear

and put their trust in the LORD.

Trustworthy

⁴Blessed is the man

who makes the LORD his trust,

who does not look to the proud,

to those who turn aside to false gods.

⁵Many, O LORD my God,

Abundant

are the wonders you have done.

Mine

The things you planned for us

no one can recount to you;

were I to speak and tell of them,

they would be too many to declare.

and thanking Him for what this particular part of His character means to you. Or you might want to write a song, sketch some cool graffiti, or draw a picture. The idea is to be creative as you talk to Him and worship Him through the words and images you write on the page. Not too artistic? You might want to draw a diagram or just journal (write out) your conversation with God.

The main thing is to make it first person, telling God how much you appreciate Him for Who He is and what He has done.

Here's a sample…

Wow, God has a lot of amazing attributes! And there are so many more.

So how will we know which attribute or characteristic to focus on for the *30-Day Journey*? Every day we will read one of the Psalms. We want you to grab your Bible and read the whole Psalm. In the *Journey* we will highlight a few verses from the Psalm you read and some of the attributes of God that are talked about in that section. For the first ten days we will all focus on the same attribute. Before days 11 and 21 you will receive more instructions, so stay tuned.

So for days 1–10 you will see the attribute you are going to focus on for the day. After that, you're on your own. You may want to write out a prayer to God about that attribute, praising Him

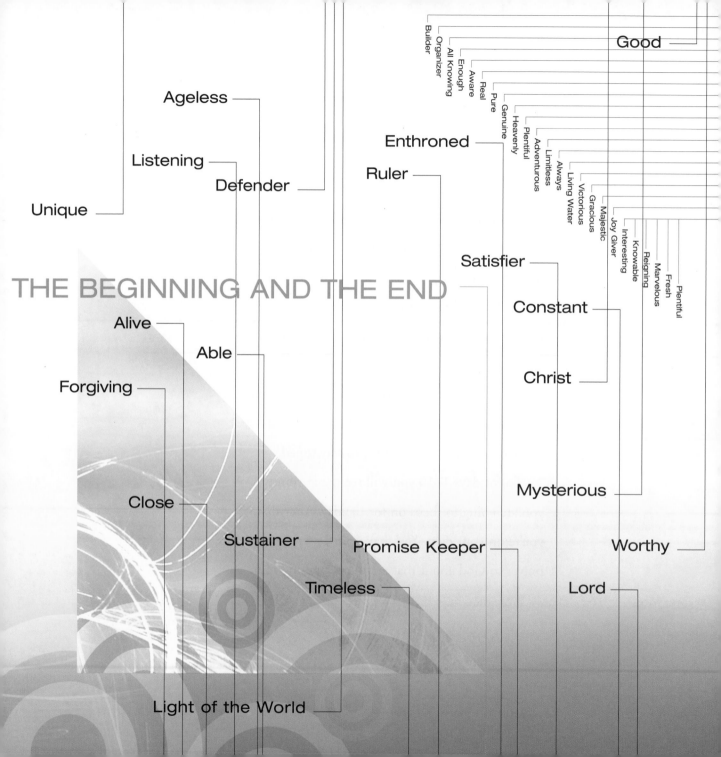

THE BEGINNING AND THE END

Unique
Ageless
Listening
Defender
Enthroned
Ruler
Builder
Organizer
All Knowing
Enough
Aware
Real
Pure
Genuine
Heavenly
Plentiful
Adventurous
Limitless
Always
Living Water
Victorious
Gracious
Majestic
Joy Giver
Interesting
Knowable
Reigning
Marvelous
Fresh
Plentiful
Good
Satisfier
Constant
Christ
Alive
Able
Forgiving
Close
Sustainer
Promise Keeper
Mysterious
Worthy
Timeless
Lord
Light of the World

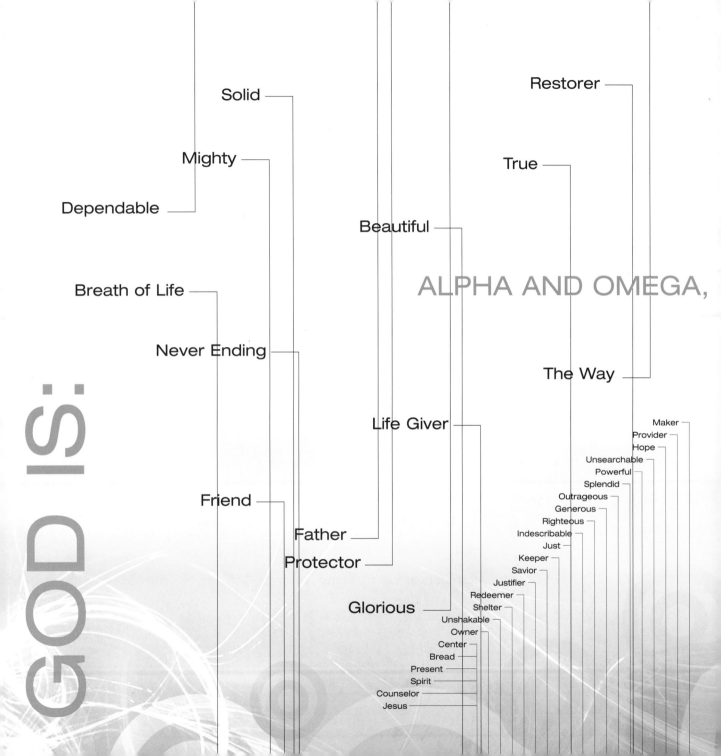

GOD IS:

Solid
Mighty
Dependable
Breath of Life
Never Ending
Friend
Father
Protector
Glorious

Beautiful
Life Giver

Restorer
True
ALPHA AND OMEGA,
The Way

Maker
Provider
Hope
Unsearchable
Powerful
Splendid
Outrageous
Generous
Righteous
Indescribable
Just
Keeper
Savior
Justifier
Redeemer
Shelter
Unshakable
Owner
Center
Bread
Present
Spirit
Counselor
Jesus

Gentle, Powerful, Love, Unchanging, Wise. . .

Good job. Obviously, there's more to God than we could fit in any book. But just to list a few more of His attributes…

We want to know everything we can about Him. And here's the best part—we're not just gathering information about God, we actually get to have a personal relationship with Him.

If you're ready, let's get started by listing as many of God's attributes as we can. An attribute is simply one of the things that is true about God, one of the aspects of His character. I'll start us off with a few, but you keep going with others you can think of.

God is: **Holy, Blameless, Kind, True, Mighty, Close, Unique, Unshakable...**

Think of it like this. While most people have heard of Maroon 5, there's always that one person who is a *super fan*. You know the person I'm talking about. They can name every band member and know everything about them. They know every word of every song on every CD, belong to the online fan club, have bookmarked the official band website, and know "all things Maroon 5!" Sure, most people have heard their songs on the radio, but this person has made it a priority to know everything they possibly can about the band.

Well, our objective isn't to get to know some rock band (Maroon 5 might not even be cool by the time you read this), but to get to know the God who made us. We don't just want to know that He's really big and that He lives in heaven.

getting to know as you begin to discover the fullness of who He is.

It's a little like freshman biology. If you've been there you know what I'm talking about—*the frog!* How can you forget? First there's the awful smell of the formaldehyde they keep it in. Yuck! Then there's the frog. No one is sure how he (or she) died, just that it's dead and now is being cut open so we can see its insides and identify all its parts. It's both gross and fascinating at the same time, but the point is this: Your knowledge of the frog can consist of knowing that it goes "Ribbet" and can jump a long way *OR* you can really know the frog by understanding its various parts and how it's made.

OK, maybe that wasn't such a good example.

But whatever aspect or facet of His character you choose, you're going to carry that characteristic of God with you all day long.

Say you start with God's faithfulness, choosing to praise Him because in every situation He remains the same. For the whole day, *Faithful* will be tattooed on your brain! Your going to chew it up, digest it, meditate on it, talk to God about it, journal some thoughts about it, think about it a little more, ponder it, respond to it, imitate it, be influenced by it, pray about it, appreciate it, and go to bed thanking God for it. You might even dream about it. And you know what? After thirty days you'll be amazed at how much better you know Him. He won't just be this huge, generic "God" to you. He'll be someone you're really

That's what the *30-Day Worship Journey* is all about. Our goal is to get to know God and to learn how to worship Him in everything we do. How are we going to do it?

1. We are going to develop a habit of worshiping God as we praise Him for thirty days.

2. We are going to know God better as we focus on individual aspects of His character every day.

Here's how it's going to happen. Each day the *Journey* will help you zero in on one part of God's character. It could be His faithfulness, patience, wisdom, or constant presence. Or that He's a perfect Father. Or a trustworthy, fair, and encouraging Savior.

OK, are you ready for this—God is inviting you to know Him. That's right, the Creator of the Universe wants to be your friend. It's the most amazing invitation you're going to receive in your lifetime and the biggest deal that's ever going to happen to you.

Sure, Bono could text you with a personal invitation to join him and the band on the next leg of the U2 tour. Or Tiger Woods could drop by the house tonight to see if you wanted to go out for a round of putt-putt. But let's face it, even if either of these things *did* actually happen to you, how could they compare with the invitation that is already yours? Through Jesus Christ you can know God intimately.

But knowing God—just like everything else in life that is worth it—requires a high price. It's no different than making the cross-country team at school or taking AP classes. Accomplishing great things demands a lot from us, and knowing the God of all Creation is no different. You don't just wake up one day with a really "tight" relationship with God just because you want to. You have to be willing to pay the price.

THIRTY-DAY WORSHIP JOURNEY

LOUIE GIGLIO

30 DAY WORSHIP

JOURNEY

MULTNOMAH PUBLISHERS® *Sisters, Oregon*